HEALING

THE

LIMINAL

HEALING
THE
LIMINAL

Lessons & Parables for Finding Your Way

MARCELLA KROLL

STERLING ETHOS
New York

STERLING ETHOS
New York

STERLING ETHOS and the distinctive Sterling Ethos logo are
registered trademarks of Sterling Publishing Co., Inc.

ISBN 978-1-4549-4873-5
ISBN 978-1-4549-5688-4 (e-book)

Library of Congress Control Number: 2024933396

For information about custom editions, special sales, and premium
purchases, please contact specialsales@unionsquareandco.com.

Printed in China

2 4 6 8 10 9 7 5 3 1

unionsquareandco.com

Cover and interior design by Stacy Wakefield Forte
Cover and interior art by Marcella Kroll

The text is set in IM Fell English. The Fell Types are digitally
reproduced by Igino Marini. www.iginomarini.com

For the wise ones we never got
to meet, by fortune or fate.
For the dreamers obscured by
survival or hate. I exist for you
even if others can't see it. I am
here in spite of others saying
I don't have a right to. I see you
in my eyes, nose, jaw, and shape.
I know you love me beyond
what small minds could make.

—LOVE,
YOUR DESCENDANT

Because I exist, I have meaning.

I belong here.

I am real, worthy of love, and whole.

*I am wanted, welcomed, well-received,
included, and invited.*

*I am valuable and more than enough
just being me.*

This is my birthright.

—CATE E. GERSTBERGER

CONTENTS

Introduction ---------------------------- ix

CHAPTER ONE. Opening the Space --------------------- 1

CHAPTER TWO. Bone and Blood---------------------- 13

CHAPTER THREE. Impact Is Greater Than Intent---------- 47

CHAPTER FOUR. Confronting the Shadow --------------- 61

CHAPTER FIVE. Staying the Course ------------------- 97

CHAPTER SIX. Mediumship and the Liminal --------- 127

CHAPTER SEVEN. Initiation-------------------------- 157

CHAPTER EIGHT. Earth and the Galactic Families -------- 187

CHAPTER NINE. Blurred Timelines------------------- 207

CHAPTER TEN. Unmasking-------------------------- 235

CHAPTER ELEVEN. Holy of the Holies ----------------- 243

Conclusion---------------------------- 253

Recommended Reading --------------- 256

Acknowledgments --------------------- 257

About the Author -------------------- 258

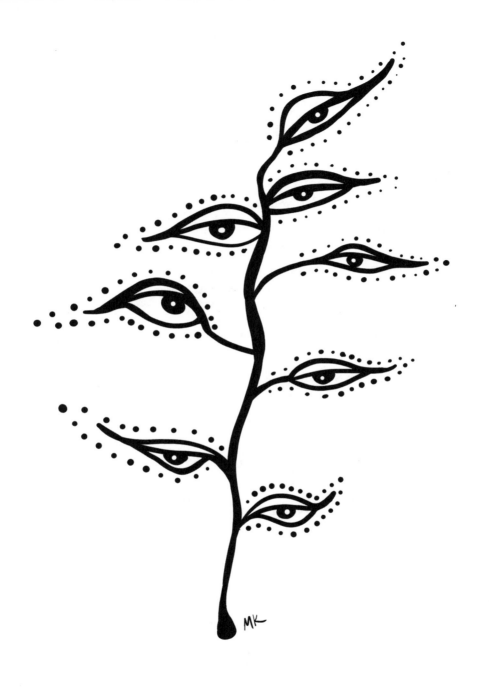

introduction

WHAT IF I TOLD YOU I WAS A DESCENDANT of Moses? Yes, that Moses. At least, that was what the Houngan (Voodoo priest) said in the *Vodou leson* reading I received from them. You may not believe me, and that's okay. I wouldn't be so sure, either. However, I stand at the intersection of converging and often conflicting bloodlines that pool together into every cell, organ, and fiber of my being. The prescription for my emotional ailments that I received in that reading was to write their stories, to channel their forgotten legacies into teachings. So I'll attempt to do just that.

I want this book to be a resource for those who felt neglected, unwanted, discarded and yet are constantly called upon to be rocks of unwavering support and resilience. I want to create a place of safety for those who felt like they didn't belong anywhere. The pressure and anxiety of the task became a voice inside myself saying, "Wow, you have a God complex for thinking that. You couldn't possibly have that kind of authority." And it's true: I cannot promise safety. But despite every attempt from the creepy little bully who tries to keep me in doubt, I have finished this book, my offering that I hope can help give even one person who feels like they don't belong a bit of peace in their spirit.

That's why the stories you will read in this book are parables, which tell a story with a moral or spiritual lesson. They are stories about those who live and have lived in the liminal space but did not have a name for it. They are stories of my ancestors, guides, and previous incarnations. We share stories so we can give them a place of reverence and the worthiness of existing. To create these stories, I went into my mediumship practice to become them, to share their story in their words but through my voice.

To live in the liminal, to me, means being neither here nor there yet everywhere all at once. To not fit in is to stand out. While that can feel like something to strive for, it can create profound loneliness for those who traverse the world when no place truly feels like home. As a multiracial and autistic person with many interests, I've often been rejected by the world around me. This rejection has come consciously and unconsciously from my peers in my community and craft, artistically and psychically, and even in my own family. Being constantly reminded that you are not enough to meet some quantifiable standard or that you have "too much" of something ambiguous or unidentifiable can pummel your self-esteem and confidence almost to nonexistence. Or worse, you might try to conform and fit in, only to have it backfire entirely and send you into the depths of your shadows. I say this all from my own experience. You, dear reader, may have feelings that differ. These are just mine. I hope that this book offers support to you in the way I wished I had received it growing up. Because as I'm discovering, a big part of my life purpose is to be the person I wanted to be there for me when I was growing up.

So yeah, back to Moses. No pressure. When the Houngan told me I was descended from Moses, at least that gave me some idea of where my clairvoyance gifts might have come from. But I digress.

Revitalizing and nourishing a lineage that has wholly forgotten itself and been suppressed, destroyed, or erased is only going to be done by channeling the stories of those who came before. Here is where I, a descendant of witches, *segnatori*, medicine people, and mediums—and maybe even, dare I even say, galactic beings—show up. While none of us may have every bit of information about our lineage, we have our flesh and blood to create a map of memories through our DNA to guide us to our healing.

So how do we heal, honor, respect, reclaim, or revise our lives and magical practices when the maps to them have been lost, eradicated, held back, or stolen? How do you heal and empower yourself when you don't have books, oral histories, elders, or really any information from your ancestral lines? Some of us also come from bloodlines by way of violence and may be too afraid to even bother trying to connect to them. We may have experienced rejection, dismissal, or exclusion from what should be our communities, where people may not have welcomed our diversity as part of the whole. That refusal can often lead to feelings of unworthiness, abandonment, and fear of being visible. We create a narrative of our feelings of not belonging. We fear being seen. How do you overcome imposter syndrome and take up space without feeling like a fraud? Part of the purpose of this book is an invitation to remain curious even when you are in discomfort or scared to approach your tenderness and vulnerability.

To do that, we will explore the idea of being okay with not knowing. This collection of thoughts, stories, and ideas aims to provide a place to connect with feelings and thought forms related to not fitting in and help you rewrite your narrative. By making space for nuance, fallibility, and healing in a nonlinear format, we allow ourselves to be messy to uncover and discover the gifts we have to offer our communities and loved ones when we show up as ourselves. We may not have all the information available, but we have our flesh, blood, and DNA to guide us through our healing. The exercises and introspections in this book give us the opportunity that our ancestors should have had while allowing us to send that healing back to them through timelines.

If you are wondering how to connect to your lineages on Earth and in the galactic to create practices that honor and respect those that came before you, then this offering is a dedication to you. Welcome this opportunity to create a practice centered on healing and offering that is just as unique as you are.

MERRIAM-WEBSTER'S DICTIONARY
MEANING OF THE WORD *LIMINAL*

1: of, relating to, or situated at a sensory threshold : barely perceptible or capable of eliciting a response

liminal visual stimuli

2 : of, relating to, or being an intermediate state, phase, or condition : IN-BETWEEN, TRANSITIONAL

. . . in the *liminal* state between life and death.
—Deborah Jowitt

chapter one

OPENING
THE SPACE

BEFORE WE BEGIN, I WANT YOU TO understand the courage it takes to dive into self-reflection. This is a reminder to commit to being your own authority. That means taking full responsibility for your own learning, healing, and sovereignty—not just in your practice, but in every part of your daily life. No guru, teacher, or influencer can fully bring you wholeness and completion. There may be a part of you that desires to find ease and grace in your self-discovery and healing, but that relief you seek can also be directly connected to your commitment and willingness to take responsibility for yourself in this process. Know that not one person—not me, not any other witch or healer—can give you all the answers and perfect remedies that will cure what troubles you.

I can make suggestions throughout this book and its parables, which are based on my unique experience, but ultimately the responsibility will be yours. I hope my journey can help you navigate your own, that it is a light that will shine on and support you. I hope that the knowledge in this book can hold a supportive and sacred space for you as you guide yourself through this process. If you don't already have a practice or a tradition of grounding, of meditation or magic—it does not matter. Not being ready or prepared should not be the thing stopping you. The only requirement for understanding the lessons in this book is being open and receptive to what is being offered and then finding the things that resonate with you. Find the ways you relate, and if there are ways that you do not connect, that is okay.

If you want to begin working with this book in a symbiotic way throughout your daily life, I recommend some helpful exercises to get you grounded in the space. You can choose to begin your experience with meditation, grounding exercises, or setting up an altar dedicated to your journey through this book, and maybe for the ones you love, too.

First, I recommend working with a twelfth-dimensional shield, which is a form of protecting and clearing your energy. The twelfth-dimensional shield activation is designed to multidimensionally ground and protect your energetic field, allowing you to discern what belongs to you and what does not.

Next, I suggest creating an altar. This will create an anchor point in your day-to-day life where you can make offerings, set prayers, or feed your ancestors and guides as you go through this process. Creating an altar is not a commitment to witchcraft. It is just another physical way to identify the work that you're doing in the invisible in a tangible physical way.

Third, learn how to create a daily grounding and energy recall practice. This does not have to be a militant meditation practice but more of a daily ritual that can lend support. It can be the little things that we do that we set up for ourselves to make us feel like we have one foot in this reality. That gives us a physical landing pad in our daily lives.

Last, I would recommend writing a declaration of intent or a personal mission statement that you would like to motivate your process.

These are just some suggestions; they are not required, but they are helpful. Following are some tips, meditations, and my recommendations for an altar, if you would like to work with them.

twelfth-dimensional shield technique

1 Let's start by taking a few deep breaths. You can find a comfortable position sitting or lying down to do this, and begin dropping into the energy point of the number zero. You can tap into this neutral starting point by taking a deep inhale through the nose and down into your solar plexus, the area just below your heart center. Then, gently release and relax your body on your exhale. Now you can state the following, aloud or quietly in your mind's eye:

MY DECLARATION OF INTENTION IS TO SERVE MY SOURCE.

I commit to serving my highest power wholly and thoroughly.

I am Source energy.

I am sovereign.

I am free.

2 To activate the twelfth-dimensional shield, begin by visualizing the Merkabah star, a tetrahedron star. Imagine a platinum six-pointed star, like the Star of David, in the center of your brain, then move your Merkabah star down through the central column of your body. You see it passing through each chakra and releasing from between your legs. Now send your six-pointed star to the center of the Earth to the Earth Star Grid, an energy center that holds a grounding frequency for the planet deep below. You can feel unconditional love and unity for all as you connect your star with the Earth star.

3 As you connect to the twelfth-dimensional platinum light, feel that light building momentum through your entire body. As you connect and fill up with the platinum energy, see your six-pointed star returning to you, and let it stop at a position twelve inches beneath your feet. As you focus on your six-pointed star, it will start to spin, build momentum, and create a platform of platinum silver light. This light is your twelfth-dimensional shield. As the protection strengthens, it will produce an upward movement of a pillar of platinum-white light. Allow that pillar of light to reach a position about three and a half feet above your head, and feel and sense your entire body encased in the twelfth-dimensional platinum-white light. Allow every cell and every pore of your body to radiate in the platinum-white light, as you focus again on that position twelve inches beneath your feet.

4 Next, visualize your six-pointed Merkabah star, and draw your Merkabah star up through the center column of your body, letting it pass through your chakra column and release out of the top of your head. Send your star to a position three and a half feet above your head. As your Merkabah star again begins to spin, see it create a shield at the top of your head. This allows your twelfth-dimensional star to create a pillar of light. Feel yourself fully encased from top to bottom in your twelfth-dimensional platinum shield.

5 Now, multidimensionally ground your shield by focusing on your six-pointed star at three and a half feet above your head. You will send your Merkabah star out toward the cosmic heart of our universe, out to Andromeda galaxy. As you connect to the universe's core, allow the crystal star to emanate its connection to you. As you feel protected and supported in your twelfth-dimensional pillar of light, say within your heart:

THANK YOU, SOURCE.

Thank you, Ascension Guides.

I am Unity.

And so it is.

declaration of intent

Words have power and can create a thread or a through line on this journey. Creating an explicit declaration of intent when embarking on this healing path is highly suggested. Why? Because by doing so, you offer an anchor and a magical compass for your energy. Navigating the liminal can bring you down paths and open doors that you didn't know were there. Having a declaration of intent can get you back to the purpose of the work.

1 Think about what you would like to achieve here with this work. What is your goal? Is it for your inner child? Is it for ancestral healing? Is it to find inner peace or ease? Is it to see more clarity or have more confidence? There is no wrong answer. You can modify your intention as you move through this journey. I recommend keeping it simple to start. Try to contain your intention in a sentence or two, not a wordy or lengthy paragraph, because we can get lost in words in the way a story can take lose its plot if it takes too many different turns. Think of this as a mission statement. Your statement will keep you from being overwhelmed by the process. Remember, you can always amend, add on, or clarify as you make your way through the process and things become more evident. For now, keep it simple to set the tone and direction for moving through this particular path of working. Some examples might include the following:

I AM A DIVINE VESSEL FOR MY HEALING.

I show up with ease and grace through my process.

*I am a vehicle for the healing and well-being of
my elevated ancestors.*

*I invite healing, revolution, and grace as I find peace
in the liminal.*

2 Make sure that what you write or create as your declaration of intent is your own and feels true to your heart. Throughout the process of working with this book, you can always change your words, redirect your attentions, or change your purpose. You can also use this declaration of intent for any area of your life, work, relationships, or creative process.

3 A declaration of intent is like setting intentions at the new or full moon. It allows you to have a visible pathway so that if you get distracted or fear arises, you can return to your intention and remember why you are here. This practice of creating an anchor through words constructs a space where distractions can fall away or leave if they no longer need to be present.

quick grounding
visualization

This quick grounding visualization can be done anywhere, anytime. You can do this in a pinch or if you are in a hurry. No special tools are required—only your imagination and visualization capabilities.

1   Take a moment to close your eyes, or keep them open if you need to. Start by bringing your awareness to the base of your spine and imagine a beautiful golden cord as wide as the spread of your hips. With your breath on your inhale, bring light, oxygen, and consciousness into your body. You can then send that breath down, deep into the base of your spine, to the seat of your soul. On your exhale, imagine that beautiful golden cord unfurling and making its way down into the center of the Earth as you breathe in consciousness energy and exhale that beautiful golden cord down to the center of the Earth. Imagine releasing any stress, tension, static noise, or energy that might be throwing you off or making you feel imbalanced or disconnected from the Earth.

2 As your beautiful golden cord locks into the center of the universe, know that you are now firmly connected to the Earth's healing energy. You can call on this connection at any point throughout your day. If you tune into this cord in the days, weeks, or years ahead and it is not a beautiful, brilliant color, you can always release it to the center of the Earth. Ask the Earth to take it, recycle it, and send that energy back into the planet for healing and regeneration. Then you can also create a new cord to connect you to that grounding energy. This visualization is a simple yet effective way to connect your energetic field to Earth's energies.

BONE AND BLOOD

YOUR ANCESTORS ARE SUPPORTING you even if you do not know their names. They are deep within your cells, bones, and blood, like an impression pressed into clay. In the same way film takes an imprint of a vision, stores it, and encodes it, the memories, mannerisms, fears, traumas, and loves of your ancestors are encoded within yours. Like a deeply programmed operating system, your habits and characteristics are your own. Still, those strange, often unexplainable knowings, fears, and cravings—maybe patterns of behavior or trauma—are all connected to your lineage. We often glamorize our ancestral line and make heroic mythologies of their existence, which is beautiful. That's how we survive: by storytelling and by remembering. However, while some of our lineage is admirable, we all also have some that is not, and we often tend to shy away from recognizing the ones who are unwell.

There are both elevated and unwell ancestors, but we often are taught to forget the troubled and not so admirable ones, and glamorize and romanticize the rest by upholding the memories only of the elevated ones in an attempt to justify or validate our existence. Some of us live in shame and fear of those unwell ancestors in our lineages. It's often an assumption that we must feel immense guilt, anger, and shame to be worthy activists or allies as accountability for what our unwell ancestors have done. While it is true that anger can be a great motivator, it is not always the best tool when confronting these deep shadow wounds around identity, especially as shame can immobilize our healing journey. While I can't speak for everyone on this, I can only speak for myself as a multiracial person who has had limited success wielding my anger in my quest for belonging.

I feel undeniable rage and upset when I think about my ancestors that caused direct harm or pain, especially when I know of the relatives (mine and others) who suffered under the painful and harmful acts of violence committed by my unwell ancestors. Still, I also know that I have my elevated ancestors within me. These elevated ones are here to help support my bloodline by creating healing and a sense of responsibility to heal any of the harm created by the unwell ones. It's imperative in this body of a multiracial person to dismantle systems that my unwell ancestors may have put into place and not to harm or further negatively impact future generations.

Sitting around in a constant existential crisis will not help the current narrative or make a difference. I can feel pain and empathize, but I cannot sit around in guilt for what they have done. That also defeats the purpose of doing the work if I am making it about me and centering myself instead of creating a space of advocacy and healing. I think some people are motivated by guilt and anger, which is fine, but I know that does not motivate me, personally—it only makes me not want to exist. This, in turn, perpetuates the cycle of erasure.

When that guilt or shame takes over, I feel like a ghost haunting this place. I've often gone through many days and months of suicidal ideation because it feels impossible to exist this way peacefully. A lot of pushback will come in the form of others telling you "You don't care enough," "You don't belong," or "You don't have a right to have a voice." These harmful assumptions bring a great discomfort in being perceived. They strike deep within feelings of not belonging, being cast into the role of an outsider, and feeling like an inhuman object.

As a product of colonization, slavery, misogyny, power, and control, I often wonder, *How do you take up space when you are continually apologizing for existing?* I'm no longer apologizing for being here. I'm done with being tokenized for the purpose of making others comfortable with my existence. I'm done with feeling immense shame and embarrassment and abandoning myself. That is the whole reason why this reality exists. There is so much pain in this existence. However, that does not mean I have to live in this shame anymore. That does not mean anyone like me or who has gone through these experiences has to suffer, not at this extreme. We can heal without suffering. It does not mean there will be no pain, but this is the invitation to heal without dragging ourselves through burning coals to make a point. We can create a new reality without toxic empathy and give ourselves the healing to move forward without martyrdom.

While I spent a significant portion of my thirties and forties focused on ancestor veneration, there came a time to release the belief that I could be fixed by connection, or what some would consider an acute obsession with them. Acknowledgment of the past is crucial. But what does staying stuck in the cycles and stories of pain and redemption do to heal those wounds? I needed to get into the present to live as a human being in today's world, not just as a vessel venerating the pain of the past—not waiting for someone to permit me to feel validated in order to move on. I had also become dangerously attached to my identity as a person engaging in ancestor veneration. Who, I wondered, would I be without this mission? My ancestors had taken up so much space in my life—not just my benevolent and healed uplifted ancestors, but my unwell ancestors too.

They held on to me the same way that a possessive friend or lover would have, preventing me from making deeper connections with others because they relied on my purpose to bring them healing.

Unbeknownst to myself, in pursuing my connection with ancestors, I had stopped myself from being fully available for deeper meaningful relationships. I had directed most of my energy to this practice of healing my family line, much in the same way that I might use drugs or alcohol to fuel my escape from this reality. I created a false sense of purpose that was not rooted in the present, existing in the moment. I denied myself pleasure and instead lived in pain, shame, and a never-ending search for redemption.

So one morning, I took my ancestral altar apart to clean it and reassess the reality of my existence. I took all of the photos and names attached to it and placed them in a drawstring gift bag. I held them in my hands, and I cried. It was a moment of recognizing them and my ability to be a good descendant.

I made them human again. I was no longer putting them on a pedestal and thinking of them as gods that dictated my life direction. In those moments, I prayed to them and assured them I was not abandoning them. Still, the reality was that I could not uphold a fully actualized spiritual connection to them and live my life as a human while connected to their reality. The healing and wanting to belong that I so desperately craved had been in front of me for some time, but while I was fixated on my relationship to ancestors, I was not ready to see it. While I'm forever grateful for the opportunity to be a vehicle and a bridge between my ancestors, I also remember coming here to this earthly plane to live.

There is a distinct comfort in staying in the liminal, when the physical reality does not seem to accept or understand you fully. And yet, it is not your time to leave this physical place. I honor and revere those unwell ancestors with parameters that I have set. When I create time and space for them, I do not allow them to dictate my life and its direction. It can be hard to put yourself first when you've been told your whole life that you are selfish and when you've only just come to realize that the only people who called you selfish wanted to control you by minimizing your power, keeping your light dim, and not fostering your growth. There can be moments of resentment when you long for a life that could have happened had you received support from the people around you. You could have also been allowed to exist to empower them. But you must grieve those old stories, narratives, and potential timelines and return to the present from where you stand now. Then give it all you've got!

HEALING THE LIMINAL ALTAR OFFERING SUGGESTIONS

Creating an altar, while not necessary, is highly suggested if you choose to journey along this adventure of the liminal. An altar does not belong to anyone religion or practice. An altar is where one comes to honor the sacred by creating a physical landmark for the unseen. The purpose of an altar is to act as a place of divinity, prayer, reverence, magic, and to be a portal to whatever its assigned intention may be. Creating an altar will help you hold space for your process, your ancestors, your guides, your divine spirit team, and any goals for which you wish to seek support.

An altar doesn't require a fancy setup. In times of desperation and being houseless in Los Angeles, I constructed a few altars on the dashboard of my car with just a napkin, a pinch of tobacco, a small crystal, and sometimes feathers I had found along my path. My only rule when constructing an altar is to treat it as a sacred space, a place that you would not desecrate with trash or disrespect and that you would not let others tamper with. Let this be your sanctuary.

No matter how simple or elaborate, an altar can give you an anchor point from the Unseen into the physical, and it can help manifest the healing and communication you seek to gain from the unseen.

Some simple suggested items for beginning a liminal space healing altar:

* A small glass of water.

* A tea light or small white votive candle.

* A skeleton key, or any key, to be used as a talisman.
  This will be charged or consecrated to take you from
  this world to the next.

* A small dish of sea salt.

* A piece of paper with your name written on it.

* A photo or image of a guide, an ancestor, or
  perhaps even an animal you feel connected to in
  your current life.

Before you set up your altar, take a moment to cleanse your
space and clear your mind. Use the grounding visualization I mentioned previously, and if you haven't used the twelfth-dimensional
shield, I recommend that as well.

Then, identify a modality for cleansing that is most appropriate for you. Begin to cleanse your space and clear your mind. I like
to light incense and play healing frequency sounds. You will then
find a place for your altar where it will not be disturbed by pry-
ing eyes, partners, family members, familiars, or roommates. You'll
want this to be only for you. Once you have found your place, you
can begin to arrange your items—the glass of water, the photo or
image, the key, the dish of sea salt—in a way that pleases you.

Write your name on a piece of paper and make a declaration of intention for the altar. You can ask your guides and guardians to keep you protected but not hidden during your journey. You can ask for support as you navigate the liminal for your understanding. You can ask whatever you like. Ensure that the intention feels true to your spirit and what you are ready to invite into your life.

Then, take the piece of paper with your name on it and place it in the bowl of salt. The salt adds a cleansing element and a warding of your name to ensure safe travel and protection for you and your guides as you process. You can keep this setup throughout your experience with this book. Or, if you feel intuitively nudged to, add additional support items like other stones, photos, or flowers. You can also assign this altar a task or name it as the portal to a specific support you need. You will know what is proper and correct for you.

ancestor veneration tree

Ancestor veneration, sometimes called veneration of the dead, has been widely practiced in many cultures for thousands of years. The belief is that honoring our ancestors allows us to stay connected to our lineages in the spirit realm and have their guidance, support, and sometimes intervention. Ancestor veneration is practiced not only out of love and respect for the deceased, but also to help continue their existence and provide direct contact for advice and support.

Ancestor veneration can be used to connect with people within your bloodline and, in honoring the ancestors and lineages of your creative field, your work, your passion, and even your religion. For example, if you are an artist and want to venerate the ancestors of your craft, you could create a practice of reverence to connect to them and petition their support. The same applies if you are a doctor, teacher, or scientist.

There are many ways to venerate your ancestors year-round, and one of the most common practices is to create an altar. But there are plenty of other ways, and I want to share one with you that helped me personally: the Ancestor Tree.

So what is the Ancestor Tree? I created the Ancestor Tree with creativity and magic when I was desperate for connection but felt that I had nowhere to begin. It begins with an image of a tree that I drew: the roots, the trunk, and many branches that rise up and extend outward.

1 First, write your name in the central column of the trunk.

2 Then, extending up through the branches, write your biological parents' names, if you know them.

3 Then, write the names of any family members whose names you know within the branches. What happens if you don't know your relatives or where your lineages descend from? I suggest writing the word *ancestor* instead of a name—you can write that over and over and over again as needed.

4 On the roots of the tree, write the names of the energy that supports you, such as people with whom you have personal relationships, like spouses, partners, children, or even good friends. Know that you can go back in and write more names as you discover or remember others.

5 Once you feel satisfied that you have filled out the tree to the best of your abilities, take that image of the Ancestor Tree and place it on your altar, if you have one. If you don't have one, that's okay. Find a place to set your drawing where it will not be disturbed. Make the tree the centerpiece of this area.

6 When I first created my Ancestor Tree, I placed it on my altar. I added some flowers, just carnations at the time. I recommend adding flowers to yours. You can choose whatever flowers you want. Some people select sentimental flowers like roses or marigolds because they attract the spirits of the dead. But anything that draws your attention will work. On my altar, I also put a glass of water for my ancestors, should they get thirsty. Then I added a little piece of chocolate. Try adding something that your ancestors would enjoy. Again, offerings are all suggestions. You can add whatever you want.

7 Another thing I like to add is a candle. Any candle will do, even if it's an electric one. I had a profound experience using the ancestor candle I got from a small business called Magic Hour Candles. I placed it next to my tree image, lit it, and then allowed it to burn for several days. After the flame finally flickered and disappeared, I received multiple emails from my Ancestry.com account. I had taken a DNA test three years prior and had completely forgotten about it. I learned that I had been matched to several new relatives, ones that I did not recognize. We didn't seem to look alike at first, but after a closer look, there was familiarity in the faces that I recognized. This process started to connect me to more names of people I had not known before. I added those names to my tree.

Did the tree work the magic and connect me to these people? Perhaps, because it gave me an anchor to bring that energy into my day-to-day reality, and that started the process of uncovering and discovering some missing puzzle pieces of my origins. I made contact with my biological father within a year of creating the Ancestor Tree. Did my drawing have something to do with me finding him? Absolutely. Did it bring me to my father? No, not entirely—but I believe it acted like a portal to that family energy. The more I received names that connected me to my father, the more they acted like an energetic bloodline link. So do with that what you will, but I have found the Ancestor Tree to be a super helpful way to ground and connect into my lineages, allowing me to create connection and possibility where there once wasn't.

Agneida, the Time Traveler

AGNEIDA ABRUPTLY awoke in an unfamiliar place and thought, *It's happening again. Quantos anos? What time is it? What year is it? Where am I?*

"Oh no, not again!" she exclaimed. She had a habit that was something like sleepwalking. But is it sleepwalking when you've already crossed over into the Land of the Dead? She was a spirit lost—constantly searching for familiarity, for her loved ones, for something recognizable. She was continually searching for a home. She had forgotten her divine assignment. Although she would have moments on the edge of remembering, she'd immediately black out when her mind seemed to edge too close. She slipped through dimensions, not quite asleep and not quite awake, not remembering where she was. She would revisit her old life, haunting it with reminiscences in hopes of finding a sense of peace. She constantly questioned herself: *Is this a dream? Did I make it all up?*

Sometimes she would fall into the future through a portal created by her descendant. Suddenly she'd find herself at an altar in the woman's bedroom. While this was helpful, there was no consistency to the traditions that prompted this occurrence. This woman, her descendant, had brought Agneida to the middle plane, but there was no one here to honor her, no one to remember her stories or call on her spirit in prayer. The longer she stayed here, the more lost she would feel. So there she was, traveling through time and space, going to sleep and waking up, conscious and unconscious again, waking up in different places in different spaces all over the world, waiting for someone to free her.

Mary's Lament

ON THE morning of her wedding, Mary awoke with eyes filled with tears as numerous as drops of water in the Mediterranean Sea. She was filled with worry: would she be a good wife, a good mother, an excellent example of a woman? She was only seventeen years old, yet she had known who her husband would be from birth. Named Giuseppe, he was sixteen years older than she was, and he was made to understand that this child would provide a way for him to keep his family secure and preserve its legacy.

This arrangement may sound cruel and sadistic in today's world, but this is just how family hierarchies operated back in the old country. Mary understood her path early on and was prepared from a young age for her eventual role as a matriarch. So, on that early summer day, she married Giuseppe and vowed to be a good and faithful Catholic wife, to have and hold, in sickness and health, 'til death do they part. She kept her promise. Her devotion to her faith was the only thing she prioritized more than her husband. If she could have been a nun, she would have chosen that path, but she knew that way had never been available to her.

She grew to love her husband and found that they had common goals that drew them closer. They eventually became best friends, partners, and companions and did learn to love each other. She was not resentful or rebellious. She was a stern mother, not full of affection but consistent and responsible. There was never a hungry mouth or tearful eye that could not be soothed with her support and understanding. The worry never left her eyes, though; that would be something she passed down to her children.

Mary bore nine children and would have had eleven had the twins not died in childbirth. She believed in God so much that she never outwardly grieved her circumstance more than a week because she thought it was part of God's plan. Her faith in the Divine was so strong that her only focus in this life, besides being a good wife and mother, was to get into heaven so she could be closer to her true love, the Holy Spirit. Every day she prayed the rosary. She was a good Catholic and rarely missed Mass— only when she was in labor, and one time when she had the flu. She was so devoted she would often take on the suffering of others in an attempt to spare her loved ones the pain of their sins. Even in times when she knew she could not control the behavior of her children or husband, she would assume the role of the martyr to keep everyone in good standing with the man upstairs. That's how strong her faith was. She believed she could save people from sin, the devil's temptations, and redemption.

In some ways, she did. Mary had enough faith for everyone—her whole family and her whole community. The village would come to her when they were sick or fell on hard times. She rejected the path of the healer in her family. Sadly, she believed that the stregas, as they were called, were part of the sinful work of the devil, even though she herself had the gift. She always had a word or a prayer to assure others that they would rise again, just like the son of the Lord.

She did have moments of doubt sometimes, but rarely. Still, she occasionally would be vexed into thinking she was foolish to be so devout, especially when harsh winters and moving to a new country would prove financially, emotionally, and physically distressing for her family. However, she always came back to her faith . . . so much so that her unwavering belief would become an annoyance to her family. However, in becoming that annoyance, her faith only grew stronger.

But no matter how much she prayed or tithed, she worried constantly. It increased to a fever pitch when her husband began making dealings that would be seen as illegal in this new world. As a good wife, she had to acquiesce to his decisions without protest. But she had one condition: she made Giuseppe promise to go to Mass and confession to be absolved of his sins. He did as she said, and funny enough, he grew fond of it. It gave him a sense of peace, which helped ease her fears and reassured her that she was indeed a good wife.

Though they lived a hard life, they gave their children all they had, including an ocean of worry, a drive to succeed, and enough audacity to do things differently. The only thing that seemed to skip a generation was a devotion to God. The children believed, but they were more afraid of the punitive side of the Lord than devoted to his ability to perform miracles.

Giuseppe died first. Her devotion to her husband was intense, but her freedom to commit to God the almighty was more vital. She left this earthly plane a year after Giuseppe's death, not sad but with happy tears in her eyes. She died knowing that she did what she was raised to do in this life, and now she could be with her Father in heaven. Her unwavering faith in a higher power, in God, could never be broken, no matter her circumstance in life. She would also pass this on in subtle ways, although more to the generations that would come after her children. Her gift was her unbreakable connection to the Divine. Her legacy was the drive to bear the worries of those around her in the act of ultimate devotion.

The Dragon

ARTHUR WAS often told he was a lot, too loud, too intense, too angry, too emotional, too quiet . . . just too damn much. He did not know that he was a dragon in human form. He was much too large to be contained in such a small body. He was filled with magic. He could make things happen almost instantaneously with his imagination. Imagine living your life one way, visible on the outside, but feeling something different inside. Perhaps this contradiction was why he was constantly hurting others with his words, his outsized reactions, his unmanageable strength. It was usually unintentional. However, the wounds he had inflicted by rejection and discomfort got the best of him as he got older. His anger often turned to implacable rage. In his childhood, he was picked on by his father and older siblings. When he could not receive love or encouragement for his abilities, he felt resentment and threw tantrums. His mother would scold him and tell him to man up, as she didn't have time for coddling, and the pain would grow.

During early adolescence, the only remedy for Arthur was to escape. He found it in music—jazz and, more specifically, Algiers jazz. He could not feel any discomfort while listening. The knots in his heart would just dissolve and melt away. Music had the medicine he needed. It was as healing as the touch of a woman, but music never told him he was too much or not enough. He daydreamed that he would open his own jazz club when he got old enough, a place where everyone who felt orphaned by God or their families could come and let the music heal them.

First, he would have to ensure he lived long enough to see that through. It's challenging enough being a dragon, but being an Afro-Indigenous man in the 1930s was bullshit. You may have had wisdom, and you may have kept your power and your freedom, but you'd still be treated like dirt under someone else's shoe. He saw it daily at his father's furniture store. It would make him furious to see his father's pride in having a business, all while his customers talked down to him. How could he possibly be proud after the government documented his whole family as colored when they were so proud to be Indigenous? Apparently they weren't Indian enough? They weren't welcome in those communities either, and it was easier to pass in those days by whatever the census called you than fight the bureaucracy and politics of any government.

Arthur could not abide by it. He also could not understand the sacrifices his parents made to raise eleven children. All he saw was the disrespect and erasure of their culture as they tried desperately to make it in a white man's world. He wasn't quiet about it either, which often got him in trouble. As he got older, he got more disgusted with the fake politeness of the people around him, feigning kindness while their disrespect was apparent. He had a reputation for being a hothead, impulsive, and a ladies' man. And yet, his ability to manifest was unmatched—even off the charts. His dragon-sized imagination still worked without fail into adulthood, and he could still make things happen so quickly that people believed in his power. But he was often too impatient to deal with the complexities of having manners, and he resisted any rules that presumed to keep him in check.

So, Arthur said fuck it to the family business and found other means to get by. Usually, they were illegal, and often they involved petty theft. But what started out small grew over time: the crimes began to escalate to burglary, robbery, and selling stolen property. There were times when he saw no harm in taking from the more fortunate, justifying it to himself by saying that he was simply trying to survive. He didn't like doing time, but he didn't mind going to jail for a few months if necessary. Sure enough, he'd be out in no time and even get a little respect for being incarcerated.

After spending a few stints in the joint, he finally saved enough cash to go in on his first nightclub. Finally, he had it: the place he had dreamed of, which could offer respite from the hostile world. He found a business partner and an investor in the only white man he trusted—no small feat—who was another neighborhood black sheep of the family. This club was the spot they would take and claim as their own. Jazz and cigar smoke filled the air, and the sweet smell of whiskey and perfumed women made all of Arthur's senses stand at attention. This moment was freedom, and this is what peace for his fiery spirit looked and felt like. He was smart, he was on top of the world, and nothing could stop him, but Lord, O Lord, did he lose all sense when a pretty woman was around. Not only did Mabel capture his attention with her looks, but the faraway feeling in her large sad eyes was something he recognized—a pain he felt without being struck. It was more than familiar; it felt like home.

Mabel was wild and free, not bound by the constructs of society. She lost her mother, Sadie, at a young age and never knew who her father was. She was not only independent—she could not be controlled. She also saw things most don't in this living world. She walked between the realms of the physical and the spiritual, and Arthur was a beacon in the darkness she felt she was constantly navigating. A knight in a shining suit, smelling of cigarettes and intrigue. She wasn't afraid of him or his fire. If anything, she was drawn to him: his magic, prowess, and power. It was like, for the first time, the awe-inspiring in each of them was revealed, and neither was intimidated or turned away from it. Arthur's larger-than-life energy made her feel seen, like anything was possible. They fell in lust at first sight and slipped into a fantasy so fast that they would forget it was still illegal for interracial marriages to exist. They found a new reality awaiting them not more than six short months after falling for each other. Mabel was only seventeen then, and she was punished for her actions by being sent to an asylum. She was pregnant with Arthur's child and had visions of the dead. Her guardians were convinced she was possessed by the devil and would not stand for it.

They sent her away immediately to have the baby alone in a home for wayward girls. Arthur was not allowed to be a part of her life at this time, and during those months, he also forgot that he was capable of being faithful. He escaped reality again by drowning himself in drink and running around with multiple women. It was sad, but even more tragic for the baby, who was left in the asylum and designated an inmate at birth.

We would hope that this love story had a happy ending and that our dragon found a way to rescue his love and raise their baby, but fairy tales are just that. Reeling from the loss of this connection in his life and thrust back into a society that starved him of human empathy, the wounded dragon could not even begin to work through the tidal waves of emotions he was feeling. It wasn't appropriate during those days for a man, let alone a person of color, to express his feelings, to show his vulnerability. He had to hide all he felt, and he became consumed by rage, anger, confusion, and abandonment. He felt betrayed by the very acts of love that once gave him reason to enjoy life. Arthur blew up everything around him, and nothing remained but the ashes of what once brought him joy. In a full-blown fire-breathing meltdown, he set his world ablaze and burned just about every bridge. He drank himself into a stupor over a few months and began behaving like a demon possessed him. He had no remorse, no care, and no shred of empathy. All he had left was fire and rage.

Arthur went into exile, back to the cave of his apartment on the other side of the river, past the railroad tracks. At first, his friends, family, and business partner sympathized, but after their attempts only resulted in more blowups, no one dared to venture back for fear of meeting his wrath. Not even his beloved Mabel could reach him. After she was released from the asylum, she tried, but he was too far gone, and she gave up, her heart broken and confused. Mabel abandoned all she had known, leaving their child with a guardian while she ran away to start a new life in another state.

Over the years, Arthur became even more set in his ways. He was sinister and abusive, spending many nights running on fumes and booze, sleeping with many women, and being volatile. He fathered another baby, and there were rumors of its death at his hand. Arthur was a hateful person with a gigantic presence—a monster. If only he had been taken care of. If only his power had been fostered for good.

Now Arthur was a son of a bitch, and this tale is not meant to put some romanticized spin on his horrific behavior. He was an abusive prick who did a lot of damage, but this story is here to tell you about what happens to dragons when you don't care for them. When you don't engage with them or show them what love is, dragons become malevolent creatures. A dragon who is loved, respected, and understood by those around them is mercy embodied. So is it nature or nurture that makes them a monster? I say it's both. We can't help but wonder what would have happened to Arthur had he been accepted—if his world had celebrated all of his magic and allowed him to embody that power. How would he have grown if he had learned to wield that fire to create tools and a life worth living, instead of as a destructive force? The odds were stacked against him. But what would have happened in a better world?

Here is the thing, though: dragons don't just get born once. They exist in lineages. Every so often, another one comes along. Each time it is born, a dragon will come to know themself and their power as the curse breaker of the lineage. You see, Arthur was my great-grandfather. There have been many times when I've met with mediums and psychics, and they told me to banish him, bind him, and cleanse myself of his bad karma. While he has his lengthy list of shortcomings, and I am aware of the atrocities that he committed, there is something I recognize in him that I see in myself. He still haunts me. I smell the smoke of his cigarettes. I feel his presence invade my space when certain types of music come on. I feel what made him alive and happy to exist. I also know what happens when you are deeply misunderstood and constantly blamed for holding too much energy, when people are scared of you because of what you are capable of. I know the way others try to kill your spirit before you grow up and eat it.

It's similar to how humans are obsessed with owning wild creatures and can't understand why they attack when they grow up. As Arthur's descendant, I didn't want to punish him or banish him from my mind. I wanted to free him and, maybe selfishly, take on this task because I no longer wanted to be burdened with his karmic debt or the residual damage of his actions. More important, though, I wanted to liberate him, because his spirit was negatively trapped and almost bound energetically to his relatives by haunting them through inherited trauma, anger issues, resentment, and pain. All of the wounds he never dealt with or took accountability for, he passed those down to his descendants, causing him to continue to wreak havoc in the lives of his living relatives. I wanted to give him one last chance to be seen as a dragon, freed from his mortal human form.

So instead of banishing him, I made him a meal—a spirit meal I felt he would like. I sat down on the floor of my studio apartment, as I didn't have a kitchen table at the time, and arranged two settings. Plate to plate and cup to cup, I set the table and invited him in, not with unconditional love but with recognition. No one, not since Mabel, had treated him with decency. Why would they? He set it up that way as a means to punish himself. We ate. I thanked him for bestowing this dragon energy on me and opened the pathway through the ethers for him to go. In front of my eyes, he morphed into a golden dragon and went out through the back door, making his way through the sagebrush and up the yucca tree, toward the sky, until I could see him no more. He left that day, and not a year later, I got my baby dragon in real life: the bearded dragon lizard I call Lord.

Over the years, I found ways to express my dragon energy through performance. I had a few bumps and lessons in the road as I learned how to control my temper when others tried to moderate my size. I was fortunate enough to play in bands a few times in my life, and on one show night, one of those bands got to play the stage in the club Arthur formerly owned. Ironically, I only found that out seventeen years after the fact. Arthur had been trying to connect to me for years, and I was so engulfed in my rage that I could not hear him.

I still sense my great-grandfather's energy occasionally. He's fiercely protective and respects and loves my artistic life, and while all cannot be forgiven for the pain or wreckage he has caused, it is no longer my job to carry his burden. That task is on him now to rectify. It is no one else's responsibility—no more descendants will be burdened with maintaining the shame of what he has done. As the next dragon in the lineage, it's my responsibility to control my fire and learn how to use it to create tools of love, peace, and healing to manifest a great life, one that he did not have the opportunity to have. It is my responsibility to be my ancestor's wildest dream.

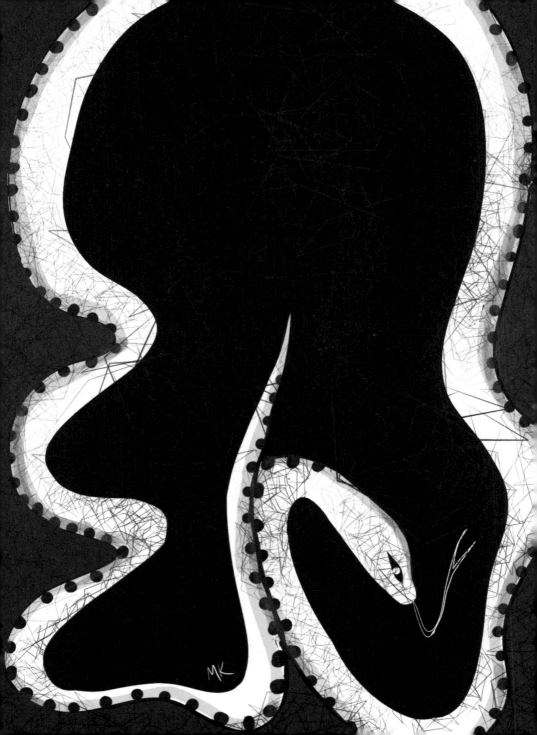

chapter three

IMPACT IS GREATER THAN INTENT

I CANNOT TELL YOU HOW MANY TIMES, even as an adult, I've been asked "What are you?" Some people ask with disdain, and some with curiosity—but the question is the same. In answer, I'll tell them about growing up and not knowing where I came from.

These are some of the most challenging and vulnerable stories I can tell, and they bring up a lot of fear for some reason, but still I'm compelled to explain my existence to these people.

When I was a tiny human, the adults around me constantly told me that I looked like a monkey. I did not look like them. I was often ordered to stay out of the sun because, as I was told, my skin would get too dark and "raise questions." Yet, I would also be made fun of for being pale. When I was eight years old, I was taken to the ear, nose, and throat doctor because my older relatives suggested that my nose was too broad and my mouth was too big. My grandmother wanted the doctor to say that I needed surgery for a deviated septum to narrow my nose. I did not understand how painful and soul-crushing that would be to my long-term self-esteem at the time. Or when my mother braided my hair and the kids would call me Pocahontas as an insult and make fun of me for looking different. They didn't know it was something their parents taught them, likely. I had long, long hair down to my butt—it was always everywhere. When I was eight years old, I had my grandmother, who taught hairdressing, cut it off and gave me a perm in another attempt to try to help me blend in.

When I was growing up, I never looked like anyone else, and people would try to guess what I "was." It was painful enough to be questioned daily about my existence. Then there is this unfortunate thing that happens when you're a child and want to fit in and start playing along. It becomes acceptable and normal to have these invasive questions asked of you, and you begin to go along with it because you are getting recognition for something.

I remember being a teenager and experimenting with makeup. I loved makeup and dressing wild. My body was beginning to take on a womanly form, and as it did, the adults started to notice and comment, usually disparagingly, about my size and weight. Thus began an eating disorder to try to look more like the girls in my grade. Around the same time, one of my uncles said I looked like a whore and brought me to the makeup counter at the mall to have the makeup people teach me how to contour my face, in an attempt to make my nose smaller and underline my lips with a lip liner to make them appear smaller. I also had braces at the time to help minimize my overbite, and what they thought was a possibility of reducing the largeness of my smile. My teeth were gigantic for the size of my head, or at least that's what the adults in my life would say.

It may seem so far away, but even in our current timeline, I've had these strange indiscretions from my peers—this fetishization with my features being different, and so not quite acceptable; the constant "What are you?" that tries to categorize me or my work. People often assume my ethnicity based on the way I look and then feel betrayed when I tell them I'm not what they thought I was. Then, at other times, I've been brought aboard by people who would prefer to tokenize my mixed race as a selling point or to run things by me for approval, to test what they might be able to get away with in front of a more visibly POC individual. Yet they don't seem to understand why I pull back from participating in their group, store, or collective when this happens. There is an undercurrent of being used: I was not white enough for the white spiritual girlies, but yet not ethnically perceivable as POC because I was too white-passing. So there I was again, not taken seriously enough or discarded, and standing again in the liminal, trying to create a space where I could take up space and give myself healing.

It's a challenge when you're constantly trying to fit in and anchor yourself into space, but I think one of the best things I've learned is summed up by the saying "When you don't fit in, you are meant to stand out." Put another way, when you don't fit in, it's time to create your own space. I've mentioned that I'm mixed and feel a solid identification with that, but I've felt so undeniably driven to connect and reconnect with those direct ancestral lines. But they don't want me either. My own blood relatives (not all of them) have a fear of erasure, appropriation, and suspicion by those I look like, yet we also look different, and understandably so. This reflection sends me back to the liminal to seek out what I can and put those puzzle pieces together—without elders, without guides.

I've had to learn how to create space for myself and others like me to create a welcoming environment. I want them to know that their healing is valid and just as important as connection with their direct ancestral lines. Microaggressions within your own family or peer spaces are more common than you may realize. The hard fact of existing as a mixed multiracial person is there's always going to be someone who's telling you what you are and what you're not, who you can be and who you are not to be. Then, in the same breath, you'll be used as a gateway for someone else's fascination or a projection of their pain.

I do not know how to avoid this problematic experience. Especially as social media becomes more prevalent, I see more lateral violence coming from individuals who are young and expecting to be treated like elders when they certainly haven't lived or been loved enough in this world. I hope that someday the stories and ideas shared out there will help anyone who has felt the whiplash of being hurt by those you trusted to care for you, whether it be relations by blood or community. May these offerings start your healing and open the path to the medicine that helps heal your spirit. I want to remind you that you are essential, so needed, and a key to the next world.

CLIQUES, COMMUNITY, COLLECTIVE

Cliques are tight groups of people who come together out of survival and usually thrive on strategy, lateral violence, hierarchy, and war tactics. I know this sounds intense, but it's honestly how they operate—you've probably had your own experience with cliques, since we begin to align ourselves into cliques at a young age. You may associate cliques with middle school and high school, when their pull tends to be the most intense as we become teens and begin to construct our identities. And for some of us, cliques become a thing you learn even before school. If you grew up in a dysfunctional household, the "us against them" mentality of the clique is very often a part of life.

A community is a broader network of relationships, which means it's less intense than a clique—it operates in a more managerial function and mostly without violence, but not without drama. Individual members still spend time working out the conflicts projected by their shadow selves by playing them out on each other.

A collective is what happens when community evolves: the network is still broad, but each autonomous individual assumes responsibility for themselves within the collective. Each member of a collective understands the gifts of individuals in their network and recognizes how they work together in unison to create a shared lived experience. There's no need for individuals in a collective to mirror the same energy as their fellow members in the way they would if they lived in a community. Instead, only their natural energy is needed to harmonize. Individuals complement each other organically, which creates an active synchronization in which the collective consciousness senses the presence of different energies and exists without being affected by the waves of each individual member's response.

So what does this mean for those living in the liminal? It means that there's always been a natural progression toward collective energy. People in the liminal may be drawn to this kind of energy, an ability to live with more ease and according to their true state of being, because they can adapt and adjust to different circumstances in a more agile way than others. In a collective, different kinds of energies can be visible without eliciting fear. Liminal beings can live without feeling like they need to avoid being punished by the unwritten rules of the community, and without the threat of retaliation from the closely aligned energy of a clique.

When I was growing up, I always tried to fit into different cliques. And while I could mask or mold myself, it was only possible for a short amount of time. I think that as an autistic person, I'm naturally good at parroting other people. But inevitably the mask cracks and falls off, and that can create a strong backlash, especially after infiltrating the boundaries of a particular group. I remember this happening intensely in high school and junior high. In those years, you are morphing, changing, experimenting, and trying to make yourself a member of one group or another to fit in and belong. At that time, and after multiple experiences of backlash after I was unable to keep masking to maintain my membership in one clique or another, I realized I needed to be more fluid. I couldn't continue to perform the correct behaviors and radiate an acceptable kind of energy without it being seen as off somehow—as if the members of the group I was trying to become a part of could see that I was trying on a very surface level. It was impossible for me to remain static and "right" within the clique I was attempting to join, because that kind of existence was so inauthentic to me.

We hear a lot of talk in spiritual, witchy, and New Age circles about collective energies: I and other divination readers, healers, and social media influencers have done collective energy readings, collective meditations, and collective healings, for example. But people often mistake community for collective, when that's not what it is. Community still has a hierarchy, but the collective does not. So when I identify the collective as a social network that is the best home for a liminal being, what am I suggesting that we strive for? Many people who reside in the liminal find comfort in collective energies because they can stop trying to fit themselves into communities that deny the full expression of their entire being.

Liminal beings often have experiences that differ from the norm, and it's sometimes easy to glamorize those experiences as being better than they were. When we seek out a place to belong, we are sometimes trying to recreate a moment, and the thing is, you can't play the exact moment more than once. You really can't. You can try to preserve some essence of it, but you cannot recreate it. So the role of those in the liminal is to come back to understanding that we can contribute collectively by being ourselves—the changing, evolving, free people we are. The act of existing as yourself brings forth energy: it allows others to be more in harmony because it enables others to do the same.

In a collective, we are creating a natural way for everyone to bring their gifts to the table without forcing productivity, profit, or any kind of agenda with an end goal in sight. The collective—a society in which everyone can be themselves without worrying about overstepping the boundaries of acceptability—creates more balance, more ease, more grace, and more connection. Community can be beautiful. However, it brings with it the burden of projection, which limits us until we can fully take responsibility for our wounds and the reactions they provoke. Communities can work for a limited period of time, but the conflicts that are natural to them make them vulnerable. If we can all work toward the collective and share the common goal of individual freedom and enjoyment, we'll be working toward a world where we can all be our most authentic selves while remaining in harmony with each other.

BREAKING THE NARRATIVE

Sometimes we think we must uphold old stories to validate the existence of things that bring us joy. Or we feel that we need to have some benchmark experience, like getting married, having children, or being a huge career success to justify the lives that we want to create. Many spiritual ideals wish you to focus on manifesting a different reality and attracting abundance. But all of these things are

temporary, and while they may provide healing, they often can be as surface-level as a Band-Aid—they can't always bring you fulfillment, a sense of inner peace, or ultimate healing. It can still feel like a part of us is missing even with all of these things present in our lives. So, for a number of us, living life in the liminal can still feel like something is missing. The only way to help remedy that missing feeling is beginning to break the narrative. This will allow us to change our story and perhaps see the ways in which we are more connected than disconnected to other beings.

The first step is to retell and re-envision our baseline experiences. This may seem like an attempt to spiritually bypass the pain of our traumatic experiences, but the goal is to see what has happened to you from a higher perspective. Breaking the narrative is not about pretending things didn't happen. It's not about gaslighting yourself. It is undoubtedly not about reimagining a different history. Its purpose is to requantify your experience from a place of empowerment.

breaking the
narrative exercise

I've created this exercise to give you an opportunity to rewrite not just one moment but three key moments, themes, or storylines in your life that have brought you to the place you are today. These are meant to allow you to explore and investigate what stories and beliefs you have considered to be true about yourself. As you go over the prompts, I invite you to re-envision the present moment by rewriting these experiences, particularly the challenging ones, from a new perspective. This is not intended to deny the past, but instead to give you the opportunity for healing by reimagining them from a place of empowerment, or by considering how things would be different had you received support or encouragement. This way you may advocate for yourself moving forward so you feel supported on your path.

1 Think of three key storylines or recurring themes in your life that bring you discomfort or suffering on some level.

2 Think of three key storylines or recurring themes that bring you joy or positive memories.

3 Think of three key storylines or recurring themes in your family history or lineages that bring you discomfort or suffering on some level.

4 Think of three key storylines or recurring themes in your family or lineages that bring you joy or positive memories.

5 Think of three key storylines or recurring themes in your generation or community that bring you discomfort or suffering on some level.

6 Think of three key storylines or recurring themes in your generation or community that bring you joy or positive memories.

This is what it takes to change your direction as you move forward. You can do this anytime. It's not a one-and-done situation. I invite you to revisit these questions and reimagine your life from a place of belonging as you do so. Reflect on how your perspective or circumstances may have shifted, or what themes are still present. You can always amend, reassess, or revise as you feel called to.

chapter four

CONFRONTING THE SHADOW

CONFRONTING OUR SHADOW IS ONE of the most ancient healing paths you can take. It is a practice that has been spoken about in various ways throughout time. Many tales document a descent into the underworld to face those hidden, vanquished, or banished parts of our psyche only to find out they are some of our greatest assets. Shadow work has gotten a lot of lip service in recent years and has experienced a surge of popularity, and at the same time it has been wildly misrepresented. Shadow work cannot be dismissed as a wound you must get over. It is not just about healing your trauma surrounding sexuality and then expressing your inner villain archetype as some kind of comeback moment by demonizing your goodness. Shadow work is, in reality, about finding a balance—and that can be downright frightening.

As I have come to know, the shadow is where the aspects of your psyche that have been deemed not worthy enough to walk with you in your day-to-day life reside. Our shadow is not visible for all to see, but it periodically peeks out through less-than-desirable interactions. It shows up to greet us through emotional outbursts or dysregulations of the nervous system. And it is mirrored back to us in the form of other people or situations that trigger us and prompt us to go into battle mode. Our shadow is the only worthy opponent deserving of our attention because it's the only one that can provide genuine healing if we face it in battle. Within those darkest parts of ourselves, we can meet with what terrorizes us most and simultaneously find our greatest strength by extending our compassion to hear what it has to say, and then give it what it needs to soothe its pain. Don't reject its presence—your shadow can teach you so much about what is hurting you at your core.

Shadow work requires preparation. It requires an ability to be accountable, because facing our shit is scary, ugly, and harrowing. It can be painful to see the things you don't like about yourself staring you in the face and to know that loving them anyway is going to be what heals you. It doesn't make sense, and it also doesn't mean you have to accept your shadow's harmful behaviors. That would be a denial of responsibility: the benefits don't come from giving the darkest part of yourself a pass, but rather in bringing those less-than-desirable attributes out into the open. They come from giving your shadow a sounding board to express those things that make you feel ashamed, uncomfortable, or unlovable. Shadow work means giving voice to these feelings and finding out why they move you to react the way you do. Remember that finding healing is not always pretty or euphoric, because it means acknowledging the ugliest nature of things and recognizing them as real.

I have also found that the shadow you've been carrying around is sometimes not just yours, but your ancestral shadow as well. Think of it like a family photo album of the ones who came before you. Family wounds that can't be healed are carried and passed down through the generations, eventually becoming a burden on the next descendant in line. We as humans create mythologies of family curses in this way. I don't think these are actual curses. They are more of an inheritance of shame and shadow within our lineages that our families avoid processing. Held onto over the years, these feelings are never dealt with. They become these repetitive cycles—narratives that, eventually, a new generation must take on until the shadow is finally confronted. Give yourself space to look at these shadows—yours, your ancestors'—and know that while we each have our demons, we are also forced to take on the weight of inherited things.

There are tools to help you connect to the shadow to find healing. You just have to remember that shadow work is not to be treated lightly, and don't expect to meet your shadow only on the surface—it will surely drag you to the underworld to meet it face-to-face. And even if you avoid meeting the shadow in this way, you can expect it to appear in your interactions with others. So you might as well find ways to equip yourself in order to take it on.

Here are some methods, both practical and magical, with which you can begin to address your shadow self, bring it to light, and send it healing:

* Write letters to your younger self to tell them how different life is today, and send them love, healing, and support.

* Write your resentments, painful memories, and sources of hurt or sadness on a piece of paper, and then burn the paper and thank these pivotal moments for their service.

* Light candles while setting the intention to bring to light any hidden feelings, beliefs, or patterns that have been holding you back or hindering you, whether consciously or unconsciously, from healing, feeling balanced, or allowing you to move forward in your life.

I also encourage you to connect with your elevated ancestors or guides to traverse the invisible path. There are many guides and figures throughout all pantheons that work in the realm of the shadow. I recommend seeking the one that can connect with you most naturally; don't call on a deity that does not feel connected to you because you think it will get the job done. The guide does not do the work; *you* do. Find one that will hold space and keep you accountable to do the work but also protect you with compassion.

The Inescapable Fear of Drowning

N ELLY FEARED water in ways one could not explain. You would think that someone afraid of water might dislike imperceivable depths and wild storm-tossed seas—places that could obviously harm her—but that wasn't all that would bring her trembling and weeping. Nelly feared not just oceans, rivers, ponds, lakes, and pools, but sinks, tubs, water fountains, and birdbaths. Cups of water. Trickling streams. Heck, she sometimes was even frightened by her tears if she cried too heavily.

When Nelly was a little girl, only four or five years old, she got in trouble for poking around where she didn't belong. All kids are curious, which is a poor combination when they are taken care of by adults who hide illegal substances in bedroom drawers. So it was: Nelly went poking around innocently, looking for some sweets, and she found a small plastic bag in the drawers encasing what looked like a delicious chocolate treat. One of her caregivers, a friend of her mother assigned to watch her and her brother, discovered her right as she was about to pop that piece of candy into her mouth. They snatched her by the arm and shouted *"Nelly, no!"* so loudly that she burst into tears. No sound came out of her mouth, but giant tears the size of a swimming pool floated to the surface of her eyes. Her vision blurred, and the heat of them as they streamed down her cheeks felt like lava burning pathways down her face. She tried to stop them, tried to contain them, and made every attempt at wiping them away, which only agitated them and made them pour from her eyes with increased intensity. Nelly experienced the unbearable agony of feeling that she had lost all sense of control. At that moment, she thought, *What if they will not stop? What if they keep coming and don't stop? What if I drown in the water of my tears?*

Nelly became a teenager. And although her phobia receded slightly, she would be periodically forced to face her trepidations about the water. For example, she could never enjoy a bath the way those fancier folk around her would. It was the era of "self-care is face masks and bubble baths!" But Nelly would internally shout *I think not!* whenever she saw an advertisement for a new product exhorting her to relax in the tub. She skillfully avoided going to swim class as an elective in high school and took up archery instead. When her peers would invite her to go to the beach, she would conveniently fall ill. She avoided the throes of teenage heartbreak and its attendant crying spells by simply avoiding her crushes altogether. She felt confident that she had found a surefire way to control the potentially devastating outcome of exposure to water. But as most things we run from tend to find us, the day came when Nelly was forced to confront her biggest fear.

One day on her way back from high school, Nelly decided to take a shortcut home via the one-way street that ran parallel to the local park. It wasn't a big park, just a little strip of land with maple trees, a weeping willow, and a large stone with an ornamental brass plaque. She had never looked at the words; she just knew they had been there for some time. In passing, something next to that rock caught her eye. "What is that?" she pondered out loud. She moved closer to look because she could swear she saw something moving. As she approached, it became apparent that it was a bird.

The tiny creature, a little sparrow, was lying on its back with one wing extended, injured. Nelly removed the scarf covering her hair and wrapped the bird up. Surely she could bring it home and find a way to heal this poor creature. Nelly felt determined to help. As she held the animal wrapped in her scarf, not too tight and not too loose, she felt so much love. In that instant, I kid you not, that bird looked Nelly right in the eyes, and she could swear she felt the same admiration from the bird that she felt for it.

Then, as quickly as she felt the love, it disappeared. The little sparrow suddenly stopped fidgeting and chirping. It was gone. It all happened so fast, too fast for Nelly to control what came next: her eyes began to erupt with tears so big, bright, and fast, you would think a dam had broken open. Uncontrollable sobs and wails filled the air as she sunk deeper into the feelings she had been avoiding for years. Nelly felt a darkness she had never known and the world around her began to collapse. Piece by piece, the physical world disappeared and turned into nothingness. Bit by bit—first the trees, then the ground, the rock monument, the sky, and then eventually, the bird in her scarf in her hand—it all evaporated. A sea of infinite black enveloped the space, consuming every bit of matter not physically connected to her.

Distracted by the beauty of this void space, it became evident that Nelly was no longer on this earth. She was floating in space. Had she, after all this time, truly died by drowning in her own tears? In the distance, she heard a faint voice distinctly saying her name. Who could that be? It wasn't her mother, but it was familiar. It wasn't her grandmother, but it sounded similar in cadence. *Oh my*, she thought. *Death is so confusing.*

The voice was getting louder and closer. She called out "Hello, who is there?" In what seemed like a flash, the ethers began to take shape and form into a woman's body. Nelly recognized her but had never met this person, yet she fully felt her energy, knew her face, and smelled her familiar scent. Without saying a word aloud, it became clear that this person was a relative, an ancestor of hers. They took each other in with their eyes and began to converse telepathically. When Nelly had a question, her relative would respond—not vocally, but by gifting the information directly into her mind almost instantaneously.

Her name was Bisi, and she was Nelly's ancestor. Bisi was a strong protector who had always been with her as a guardian and guide from her lineage. Nelly asked her if she, too, was now dead and was to join her. To this, Bisi replied telepathically with images. She showed Nelly moments from her life, all the times she chose to excuse herself from things out of fear. Nelly saw herself avoiding the water because of her intense phobia of drowning. Bisi continued to share these images, reminding Nelly that there were times when she missed out on the fullness of existence because of these fears.

Bisi shared because she believed, in some ways, that she was at fault. Bisi began to show Nelly the tragedy that led her to the spirit world. She showed her life as a young woman, embodied and empowered in her homelands, surrounded by family and a thriving community—a life painfully disrupted by invaders. Rumors had only been present a short while, but the signs of something terrible coming had been in the skies and omens for some time. Bisi, her five children, and other relatives were taken captive and herded into the bottom of large vessels. Many voices cried out amid the clamor of whips cracking and wood breaking. Screaming, wailing, and moaning filled the air. Distressed and separated from her children and family, Bisi did not want to live anymore. She did not care for the rumors that others below deck shared, their bodies pressed against hers in the dark and heavy air. The longer this journey took, the more dead in the bottom of the ship there would be—and when someone above couldn't stand the stink, they would dump them into the sea. It was horrifying. Bisi also wondered how to find her children if she made it to wherever this ship was taking them.

Then the unthinkable happened. Suddenly explosions rocked the air above deck, and shouting began—it seemed to go on for hours, until there was no sound, just the smell of explosive powder and fire burning. It was so quiet you could only hear the wind and water. For those in the hull of the ship, it didn't take long to realize that their captors had become victims themselves of another crime: piracy. And there were leaks in the boat from the attacks. Now, everyone enslaved below would die a slow death as the ship sank to the ocean's depths. Bisi died in agony and without knowing where her children were. How could a fate worse than this be possible?

However, a few of Bisi's children did complete the agonizing journey. The same children would go on to experience the atrocities of slavery in the Americas. They would bear their own children, who would live to see freedom from slavery and segregation, and they would fight for reparations. And their children would be born as Nelly's ancestors, grandmother, and mother. This lineage was almost erased, wiped out by colonialism and slavery—but also by drowning. At this moment, Nelly understood her fear of drowning, a deeply embedded trauma inherited from those brutal moments her great ancestor Bisi experienced.

Bisi had been with her since birth as her guardian and a protector from the other side. And without knowing that it was happening, Bisi also shared her pain of that memory over and over again with Nelly—so much so that Nelly carried this pain. After their meeting, the time had come not to forget what happened, but to no longer accept the inheritance of pain. Bisi loved her descendants so much. And though she did not want them to forget the unimaginable cruelties others were capable of, she also did not want to see them hurt. So in her pursuit of justice for those responsible for such atrocities, she made a promise. She vowed that her spirit would not rest until all her descendants ceased to exist. She would be their ally and confidant in the spirit realm, protecting them from those evils. Eventually, this type of protection can become a prison of fear—this she could now see. So Bisi resolved to communicate with her great descendant and let her know that she would not drown. She would liberate Nelly from the cycle of degradation created by the actions of her captors. She would show Nelly that she could move with freedom of spirit and the full courage it takes to walk this earth with her gifts visible and the strength of her lineages supporting her, not holding her back. In Nelly's deep anguish over the sparrow's death, Bisi reached out through the void of time to communicate this message.

What had felt like hours were mere moments, and Nelly awoke to consciousness in the park. She was still holding the tiny sparrow wrapped in her scarf in her hand but sitting on the ground with her back against the monument rock. In disbelief, Nelly wondered, *Did I hit my head? Was that a dream?* She looked down at the little bird and sighed, and for the first time, noticed the plaque on the rock monument. It declared the site a homage to the enslaved Black people, freedmen, and Native Americans who helped repel the advancement of British forces in 1778. Somehow, she knew that was she had experienced was not a dream.

Nelly found a place by the oak tree and began to dig a little bit of earth out of the ground. She wrapped her friend, the sparrow, up completely and placed them in the hole she had made. Returning them to the earth, she thanked the sparrow for their help in guiding her to her ancestor and promised never to forget them. And for the first time, she shed tears without fear of drowning, collecting them with her hands and gently placing them on the ground as offerings. From that moment on, she committed to honoring those who came before her without fear of the intensity of her emotions.

Sincere Sadie

I T WAS a crisp morning, and the gusty wind woke
Sadie up abruptly as it penetrated her bedroom
window, jolting her upright in bed. Everything felt loud.
The birds chirped, the village children played nearby, and
even the sunrise felt like it had something to say. She met
the morning with wondering what the point was. She also
often questioned things most people did not dare, like if
there was a way to lay out her bones before her, the way
you would lay out an outfit the night before an important
event? Sometimes being in this body was so painful,
physically, mentally, and emotionally. Sadie wondered
how she would manage to move forward at all.

There are so many veils between this world and the
next. Why, she pondered, do people assume life has no

mystery once you have the truth? When faced with this question, her mother would say, "Why do you want to know the truth about everything?" To this, Sadie replied, "The truth is everything! Why do you want to make everything a secret?"

Thus began a lifetime of trying to unravel secrets, and a lifetime of trouble. Sadie saw the irony in the maxim to always tell the truth, since it seemed like no one around her could. She keenly observed the failings of everyone and all the things they would hide, not just from each other but from themselves. She could sense the sounds, sights, and stuff underneath the surface—so much so that they threatened to institutionalize her.

But, as much as she excelled in revealing unspeakable things to those who were unprepared to hear about them, she was also adept at finding the right words to break someone out of their shell or bring healing at just the right time. Her peers often scoffed at her sincerity because they couldn't believe her sweetness in the face of the malice of this world. Sadie could not understand the social cues of these people, who would declare their moral uprightness but lie in the next breath. These things always troubled her.

As soon as she could, Sadie set off on her adventure. Her family didn't understand her. They didn't want to understand her. They liked conformity and convention and did not like being challenged or confronted with differences. So she ran away. She found love with someone who would let her be free. He was much older, but sadly none the wiser. He wanted to keep Sadie caged like a bird because she was charming and beautiful to look at, but he didn't like the way she spoke. At first, he found it entertaining, but he was not pleased when he realized her keen observations could be used to lay bare his shortcomings. Suddenly he didn't like her rebellious attitude. Her passion for justice was once alluring to him, but only when it did not directly affect him, and his love curdled.

So Sadie left the person who provided her initial release because she knew that she would die of a broken spirit if she stayed and conformed to his desires. She traveled with a sideshow for some time as an assistant to a knife thrower. This new lifestyle satisfied her wanderlust. She was never afraid of what people told her to be frightened of, and she saw excitement in this place where others only projected their horror.

In the years that followed, she reconnected with her younger brother. She found that he had her talents for truth-telling and calling people out. The difference was that he was a man. He could move through this world without being questioned as much. And from him, she learned that she had evaded institutionalization by her family members at the last minute—had she not left town, they would have been committed. Still, the fate of punishment by being deemed insane would not escape the family line.

Sadie had two children, one with her first husband and a second with another person that she refused to name. The night before her twenty-seventh birthday, she and her brother set off on a ride in the car. Motor vehicles were a relatively new phenomenon then. No one knows what happened, but there was a crash. The vehicle was found on the side of the road about a mile away from home, wrapped around a tree. Neither of them survived. You may think this is a sad, unfortunate story. Some would think Sadie's was a lonely existence. But the truth is that Sadie lived in between, just as she wished—in a place where she could be her most authentic self. Sadie lived her truth, and no one could confine her.

Legacy of the Unlovable

E DDIE WAS brave. Eddie was wise. He won honors, trophies, medals, rewards, and awards, including a Purple Heart and a Bronze Star for being injured and for acts of bravery during World War II. He was a hero in many ways and was never afraid of the things most people were scared of. Everything he touched turned to gold, and he was good at everything he tried—exceptional even. Everything except relationships, that is. This wound stemmed from a solemn vow to be unlovable. It was so deep he would pass it down to his descendants, along with his bravery, showmanship, and excellent deduction skills.

So where did Eddie's belief in his unlovability come from? Eddie came from a long line of fishermen, sailors, and pirates. He also came into contact with a cryptid during his formative years that would cause a tear in his psyche that lasted a lifetime. A cryptid is an obscure creature, undocumented by science, usually with supernatural abilities. Some people believe seeing a cryptid is a rare occurrence. However, once your eyes are open to seeing the impossible, you become more susceptible to seeing things in all dimensions. Such was the case for Eddie.

Eddie spent most days as a young man hanging out by the docks and cleaning up the boats where his father and uncles spent most of their time earning a living. Everyone had to earn their keep as soon as they were old enough to contribute. The men of the families would go out for months on the lobster and whaling boats, exploring the high seas and spending their days fishing and hunting for the biggest catches they could find. All hoped to earn enough to support their households throughout the year financially. Many families that immigrated to the small New England town of New Bedford, Massachusetts, were originally from the Azores and Cape Verdean islands off the coast of Portugal. Since it was the first port of call, most ships took on supplies and crew from these islands off the coast, sparking a wave of Portuguese settlers arriving in New Bedford as early as the eighteenth century. While the men were off at sea, the women tended to the households, rearing children and working in mill factories that produced textiles for the garment industry. While some spent their lives this way, not all found this more traditional way of life suitable.

The proximity to the port also allowed another profession to thrive here, perhaps the oldest profession in the history of time. That is the life and art of the prostitute—a woman who exchanges sexual favors for currency. On the edge of the water right by the docks, there was a large house, dubbed the Ark by locals, with the most precarious foundation. It was a house built on top of an old whaling boat that was too dysfunctional to be used at sea. One would marvel at the sheer mechanics of how this vessel could remain upright and not float out to sea when the tide would rise. It was kept upright by blocks made of timber and steel. A four-foot-wide walkway circled the building, and one set of stairs could grant you access aboard.

Initially, the former occupants were just transient folks who had met with hard times. However, as time passed, the residents who made shelter here became less family-oriented, and the vessel was turned into a brothel and residence for those deemed unsuitable for society. This change in residents wasn't surprising, as the neighborhood in this part of town turned increasingly seedier with time. Crime began to increase as those with fewer means just trying to get by would steal from those more fortunate. Robberies would become a regular occurrence by those docks, so you had to keep your wits about you.

As Eddie grew older, he would spend more time at the docks keeping an eye on things, ensuring the boats were secure and not broken into. Over time he started to become familiar with the faces and personalities of the neighborhood and even would enjoy conversation with them. He became one of the more trusted longshoremen to work there. It was easy for him to see they were just people like him and his family, trying to make ends meet and get by. That was the thing with Eddie: he never judged anyone based on how they earned a living but more by how they treated others.

As the seasons changed and the fishing vessels returned from being gone for a month at a time, you would see the ladies from the Ark make their way out to the vessel's walkway in their loveliest dresses. They would come out and wave at the sailors returning to the docks. The wind in their hair, blowing their skirts around, revealed glimpses of a thigh, welcoming them home and beckoning them to spend some time in their company before they went home to their families. A few would even play music and dance to entice them. The strumming of guitars, sometimes accompanied by an accordion, would fill the air. Some men would throw some coin in appreciation of the music, and some would stay longer for the desired female company. It was always like a little feast upon returning home.

One evening after a full day of this variety of welcome party, Eddie's life would change. Three lobster boats arrived first, and all was business as usual. Eddie anticipated a short day of unloading followed by the usual revelry. But then the whaling vessel arrived. Looming like a ghost ship, it seemed to be stuck at the horizon. Its advance was so slow. Most of the workingmen did not want to wait for its arrival, not knowing how long it would take. Eddie told them not to worry, that he would stay. So the other dockers went home for the day or were entertained nearby on the Ark. Several hours passed before the massive whaling boat seemed to drift to the shoreline. Eddie didn't recognize the vessel and wondered, *Geez, how long have they been out to sea?* As the sailors disembarked one by one, each face looked paler and paler, eyes vacant, and they seemed to be in a zombie-like trance. The men were so distressed that they didn't even unload their catch. It was like whatever horrors they witnessed were too much to bear. Barely a word was spoken, which was unusual, as sailors are known for telling tall tales. It was as though they were ghosts of themselves. Hell, the boat looked like a haunted house on the water.

As the crew passed Eddie, barely acknowledging him, he called out, asking if they would unload their catch, but no one responded. *Well, this is just the pits,* Eddie thought as he made his way onboard to do the heavy lifting himself. Much to his surprise, he couldn't find any evidence of any catch on the ship. There was nothing but what looked like the remnants of a blood-bath or a war onboard. The only sounds to be heard were the ocean water lapping against the ships and the docks, and the occasional seagulls squawking as they fought over food scraps on the shoreline. The ship creaked as it gently rocked with the incoming tide rising. No sooner than he thought to himself, *What happened here?* Eddie heard a faint cry, almost whimpering, coming from below the deck.

The last glimmer of sunlight shone through the cracks of the wood, casting a shadow of a shape—there was indeed someone below. His footsteps creaked he made his way down, following the sound of the cries through the galley, into the captain's cabin, and into the afterhold (where you would typically find supplies), he made a surprising discovery. Before him, in the belly of this ship, was a woman held captive in what can only be described as a water tank created out of the remnants of wooden barrels meant to store oil. Iron chains with iron shackles enclosed the wrists and neck of this creature. She had a woman's head—arms, breasts, and torso—but from the waist down, the elongated tail of a fish. The scales on this tail were bluish-green with hints of purple and a silver shimmer that caught the light. Her eyes were large and dark, and her gaze carried an incredible sadness. As he looked around, he began to notice the piles of bones of men around the room. No sooner than he thought, *What on earth* . . . he began to hear the creature start to hum and coo. A sweet song filled the room. It was at that moment he knew what she was: a siren, the kind sailors and pirates tell tales of. Their songs lure men to their deaths, making them food for these monsters deep below in the ocean waters. Eddie was frightened for the first time in his life as he caught a glimpse of her razor-like teeth when she opened her mouth to sing a note he had never heard. Her song enticed but also paralyzed him physically. He was entranced but could not move. She spoke to him through her large glassy eyes. She was showing him images of what had happened to her.

In an attempt to find food for her family, which was becoming less and less possible since the greediness of man had led to overfishing the ocean, she began swimming closer to shore. She started hunting humans for food. It was a means of adaptation and survival, that was all. Men did not respect the circle of life on land, and now they were upsetting the delicate balance within the waters of oceans, lakes, and streams. The sirens were slowly dying off, and they had to learn to adapt quickly to survive.

The siren communicated that not only had her kind begun capturing men for sustenance, but they now had to start procreating with them to avoid extinction. They learned to shapeshift and live on land part-time with humans. Some sirens had even found their way onto the Ark, trying to make a life for themselves in plain sight. However, some sirens became so resentful that this was the new reality for them they broke off into different factions and vowed to kill all men if they crossed paths. They would not dare mate with the humans. This fight for resources sparked many battles between humans and sirens at sea. They were always leading each other to death, either by song or by a spear.

This vessel was no different. The crew made it a mission to hunt sirens and turn them into trophies by casting them in iron and placing them on the bows of their ships. This crew killed everyone in her family, and she was held captive, slated to become a trophy, dipped in iron, and sold to the highest bidder. However, they underestimated her abilities. She killed their captain with her song and showed them each their frightening demise in her large glassy eyes, sending most of the crew into madness. Eddie was overcome with grief as she shared her story with him, not only the history of her kind but the capture she found herself in. He empathized with and understood the loss of her family and her freedom.

Overcome with sorrow, he felt an unbearable sadness, which overtook his whole body. Even though her mission was to kill all humans as revenge and retribution, the siren realized there was a more significant opportunity in this interaction. In exchange for his life, she decided she would enact a slow revenge as punishment for the actions of the sailors that killed off her family. She let Eddie live that day, something a siren never does. But, in sparing his life, she required a sacrifice. She asked him to free her and then take on the burden of redemption for the actions caused by the sailors that killed her family. The only thing that would break that curse would be his willing abandonment of the ability to be loved, which would free his descendants from her punishing wrath.

She warned him that a failure to keep his promise would result in painful consequences to his health; this curse would continue upon his family and even his courage would be taken if he betrayed her. Without hesitation, Eddie agreed, although he didn't truly understand the impact this decision would have on his future life. That evening after the sun went down, he returned to the boat and freed the captive siren, who kept her promise and spared his life.

As the years went by, life by the docks began to change. The evolution of technology and modern invention meant more efficiency and fewer people. The Ark was demolished. Eddie joined the military and left behind the seafaring life. Over time, he found himself in a few relationships, but he could never fully embrace them because of his long-ago promise to the siren. He never told a soul about the pact he made with her. Nor did he forget it.

After the war, Eddie found himself back in the neighborhood where he grew up. His energy was infectious, and word got around that the hero was back in town. Since he was single and never married, many women flocked to him, hoping to win his affection. But the more they showed desire, the less he showed interest. Though he was lonely, Eddie never forgot his promise to the siren. He balanced his time between his family and a wilder life going out nightly, dancing, and being the life of the party. One evening, he noticed a group of young people hanging out in the corner of a nightclub he didn't recognize. As he made his way over to introduce himself, he saw her: a woman who looked familiar to him, although he had never seen her before. Their eyes met. Some call this "love at first sight," but this was something more.

Eddie beelined right toward the brunette with the bobbed haircut. "Hi," he said, "I'm Ed . . ." She interrupted and said, "I know who you are. I'm Theresa, and I'm not interested." She turned away from him. The crowd of onlookers started laughing. Eddie was immediately embarrassed . . . but also intrigued. As it turned out, Theresa was there reluctantly after being dragged by her sister Margaret, who wanted to go dancing at this popular spot because of its more rebellious crowd. The last thing Theresa was interested in was meeting a romantic partner. In fact, from an early age, she always imagined becoming a nun and never marrying. It wasn't her dream to be someone's domesticated housekeeper and cook. She barely liked doing it for her eight siblings. Eddie was immediately enchanted and spent the rest of the evening trying to get her attention, but she was unimpressed. This cat-and-mouse interaction went on for the next few weeks. Theresa and her sisters went to the club each weekend to dance and show off the matching outfits they sewed. Eddie would show up each week and try his best to impress Theresa and capture some of her attention. While reluctant, his charms and persistence began to warm her cool exterior. Soon before long, she would find him occupying her thoughts and heart. That was the summer she, the girl who never thought she would love, found it through the charms of this charismatic man who had won the hearts of so many but never seemed to be able to receive it. This development surprised Eddie as well. He didn't think he could love or be loved by another because of the promise he made those years before to the siren. The deeper he fell in love with Theresa, the happier he became, but the more physical ailments he began to have. It didn't make sense, as he was always a strong and vital man.

Around the time he met Theresa, a rumor began that a sea creature was lurking on the docks, somehow linked to the mysterious disappearances of men who had strayed too close to the shore. Eddie knew what this meant: the siren had returned to land. But for what reason? He had kept his promise. So why was she back? He needed to know, so he headed down to the water late one night to find out. As he approached the rocky shoreline, he saw her perched on a jetty, feasting on a town drunkard who got too close to the water's edge. Blood spilled over the rocks as his lifeless body lay before her. It was a mess. How could this be happening? They had an agreement. She was eager to see Eddie approach her and remind him of his promise. It was then he realized: he had believed he was unlovable and willingly assumed his life as someone who could not participate in love, but he was lovable in every sense of the word. Theresa loved him, and he loved her. His relationship would bring the killing back and disrupt the balance between the sirens and humans. The siren reminded him that failure to keep his commitment to the sacrifice would disrupt his ability to be fearless and slowly take away his health and vitality. Should he break his promise to be unlovable, suffering would come to his lineage. The siren began to smile, blood dripping from her teeth, and Eddie let out a silent scream. Eddie fled what felt like a bad dream in horror.

That week Eddie insisted that he and Theresa get married and move to the West Coast. He insisted he could get work out in California, and they could start a new life away from familiar things. He convinced himself he could outrun the consequences of breaking his vow to the siren. He never told Theresa about the promise he made to the siren. Shortly after they hit the road, Theresa realized she was pregnant. All appeared picturesque from the outside: the newlyweds and their newborn baby living the California dream. However, things slowly began to become troublesome for the couple. It was a short-lived dream, being in Santa Barbara. After a few months, the family moved back east to be closer to family and secure work. The only silver lining was that their struggles brought them closer. They were more in love than ever, and they felt that it was them against the world. But in the back of his mind, Eddie was haunted by the consequences of his broken promise.

The more he loved his family, the more pain he felt, but he didn't dare share his daily aches with another soul. However, the more his family loved him, the more his health deteriorated. Unable to keep his promise, the time came for him to pay the price: after three short years with his beloved wife and daughter, Eddie died of a heart attack, likely caused by the heartbreak of grieving his family while still alive. He knew he would have to leave his new wife and child on their own to inherit his vow, unbeknownst to them and their future descendants. The only way to be free of this pact would come the day when a granddaughter would sacrifice having children herself to stop this legacy of the unlovable.

That's the thing with inheritance: you don't just acquire the pleasant stuff. You also get the defects, consequences, and repercussions of those who came before you. Especially if you don't learn how to heal the pain lurking in the shadow of legacy. Family shadows don't start as some monster hunting down the members of a family tree. They begin as hurt, shame, or regret, creating a wound that no one tends to. Often ignored and rejected, that emotion gets shoved under a rug, into a closet, or buried under a house, where it is meant to disappear. No one talks about it, so the voice of that pain starts to become louder, even as we plug our ears and close our eyes. We ignore it and hope that it ceases to exist. But the longer a wound is not dealt with, the more it becomes infested with energetic mold and rot. Suddenly you have a family curse. However, the real issue is that those histories, pacts, inherited contracts, and historical trauma must be confronted and addressed by someone who has had enough of being haunted by some indeterminate pain they don't understand because no one in the family talked about it. Eventually, someone gets tired of suffering and playing the victim role and summons the courage to face this mythological fate monster.

chapter five

STAYING THE COURSE

DOES THIS WORK GET EASIER? SOME-
times. Then, on other days, it's like threading a needle
blindfolded with winter gloves on. When you are trying
to find where you belong, and there hasn't been a place
created for you, it can feel incredibly challenging to stay
the course and remain motivated. You will have ups and
downs. Sometimes, you will feel so excited and thrilled

with your findings. Then, your hopes will be dashed, and you will be tempted to completely lose faith in the process. There will be days when you will want to throw it all away, but you're so far away from what was familiar and comfortable that you're unsure of how to go back.

Pace yourself. Take your time. I've realized that often when I felt like I wanted to quit altogether, I didn't *really* want to quit. It was more that I needed a break. Remember that you cannot force information to come to you before it is available. We cannot force our psychic senses to reveal things to us. If we don't get the answers we're searching for, that may mean that we are not ready to process it just yet. I believe that our bodies and brains have a self-preservation mechanism that goes beyond our trauma and knows when it is the right time to take in certain information. Even if we cannot comprehend it, we can receive it. And humans in modern society have gotten very comfortable with having things on demand with the click of a button, so it can still be hard to think you want to know something—hell, even *need* to know—and then find that information withheld from you.

There is pressure to have yourself all figured out and wrapped up neatly in a bow so you can get on with your life. But I'm here to tell you that it does not matter: you will never have it all figured out. Does this mean you should stop trying to understand how to make a place for yourself in this world? Absolutely not! I think it is crucial for those who identify with the liminal and do not feel firmly anchored in a region of society to search for and create those spaces. That's the very reason why I'm writing this book. If we do not create those spaces, those stories, those anchors in this world, they can be lost. We can't just keep going around haunting this world, being seen but not heard. There are too many of us. Yes, there are days when I want to fit in, be normal, and forget everything, including how different I am. However, I've done that in so many painful ways, and on so many occasions, and it has always backfired on me.

For example, when I was a teenager, I tried desperately to fit in with what I perceived as the cool crowd. They were all upper-middle-class kids. They had nice cars, fashionable clothes, and parents who worked nine-to-five jobs. They all hung out together in packs, which always intrigued me. I always saw it as a measure of safety that they operated as a sum of the whole, and I desperately wanted to fit in. So, in an attempt to fit in, I got two jobs—not one, but two. This way, I could buy my own clothes and not wear my older cousins' hand-me-downs. I got my hair done the same way as the cool kids. I started listening to the same music, smoking, and speaking the same dialect. I was able to pass for a while. I used this manner of costume to create an identity that helped me blend in with what I saw around me. But while I could pull it off temporarily, these attempts to normalize myself always had a way of backfiring. I remember being at a party with all of these people when I was sixteen years old, and I started drinking. This was not uncommon, as I started drinking at fourteen years old. But as I drank, I began to slip out of the character I had created for myself. I blacked out and started to get sick, and who knows what else. Suddenly, I found myself heaving in the corner of a room. I was vomiting on the carpet of one of these popular kids' homes, and at the same time, I knew the mask was melting off my face. I could no longer hide my vulnerability or the truth about who I was. Then in that pivotal moment, when I was seen for the first time by these people who I thought were my friends and peers, I saw the truth. They were horrified. I was ridiculed and ostracized. There was so much shame. Those weren't my friends, and this wasn't my pack. I was then reminded, full force, how alone and weird I was.

Yes, teenagers can be cruel, but also they can be kind. I've seen it. As an aunt and a teacher of teens, I have seen the kindness that only those who have experienced the consequences of being different can show to others. We—those who reside in the liminal—must consciously practice that kindness. We must be examples of how to show up. We can hold supportive containers to create spaces where we allow others to be accountable, to be fallible, and to make mistakes. More important, we can create places where we are revered and celebrated for being ourselves—where we can contribute and not be demonized or punished for it because we are different. So, I implore you, if you feel so inclined: find comfort in not belonging, honor your unique expression in a way that is noticeable to others, and know that you have value. Even if you are not categorizable by mainstream society, even if you are how I was as a child, it makes a difference. In school, I would permanently mark "other" when asked to categorize myself. Enjoy being "other"—not out of rebellion, but because it allows you to honor all those beautiful parts of yourself so that others may do the same.

IMPOSTER SYNDROME

Sometimes we can feel lost in the liminal and inadequately mistake that for not having a place in this world. We may develop a savior complex, telling ourselves that we are destined to do something meaningful—then, we fall on our faces because it's not the path we are supposed to take. I'm not saying that we can't have a meaningful direction and help others. We absolutely can and should, but it usually stems from feeling inadequate, and the fear of being disposable. Because of the cruelty of others, we feel driven. One moment we can feel focused and confident in our direction and then, suddenly, be triggered into full-on imposter syndrome about our purpose, past, present, future, and whole existence.

Some will say you feel this way because you are not grounded enough. Some will tell you to eat root vegetables, do yoga, meditate—and you can do all those things to put a Band-Aid on those feelings—but they don't help you feel like you belong. Then the same people will tell you that you aren't living in the present, but I will tell you that is because we are nowhere and everywhere at once, and that shouldn't be perceived as a deficit or a punishment. Not every human can naturally position themself in other people's shoes and have genuine empathy for them. That is one of the gifts of being a liminal person. One of the most beautiful things I have found about residing in the in-between spaces is that you don't belong in one specific place. Still, it took me until my forty-fifth year in this body to understand that it means I have omnipresence. Living in the liminal means having an all-access pass to be able to see and go places not everyone can.

I've been very fortunate in my work as a tarot reader and a spiritual medium to connect with all walks of life. Because I am a person who resides in the liminal, there is neutrality here, or a feeling of being on hallowed ground. Being in the liminal is where nothing and everything can exist, a place where you can see the sacredness in all things even if others cannot see or appreciate it. I've seen all walks of life. Many different individuals have sat across from me in sessions, whether at the table or on the other side of the screen: all faiths, all identifications. They felt comfort in knowing they could be heard, understood, and held. So again, it's taken me a long time to appreciate the multi-pass I have, and I wish there had been someone around during those early years to help me understand the gift that this was. I wish I could have told myself that there would be people who would shut me down and hurt my spirit because of their discomfort—usually because I could see what they were hiding or afraid of. We often hear that people project or create a mirror, which is true. They get blamed for triggering other people's wounds and insecurities.

There could be thousands of voices telling you who you are and who you're not, and planting seeds of doubt (consciously and sometimes unknowingly based on their insecurities). The critical thing to remember in the cacophony of their echoes is that it is possible to find your footing and connect to all you are in your most empowering and authentic place to your truest self. When you do, you give others the courage to do the same, not because you told them to, but because you showed them by being a real-life living example, fully yourself and unapologetic.

BEING ON YOUR OWN SIDE

I first learned to sacrifice curiosity for survival as early as back as the womb. The earliest memories that I have are from deep inside my mother. I could feel it when my spirit entered my developing physical vessel. I was aware of exploring my outstretched limbs and feeling consciousness extend through them. The symbiotic nature of breathing with another human is when the reality of first contact with my mother hit me. It says so much about the dynamic of our relationship. As my legs and arms moved, wiggled, and felt breath, I began to reach beyond my form. I felt a wave of heat and fear simultaneously, and then a loud voice reverberated through my whole body. This was the sound was of my mother as she yelled "Stop it!" The first words, the first command, were filled with an intensity I had not known but would come to be intimately acquainted with as I grew up.

The reality was that I made my mother confront things she was in denial about. In my excitement to connect, instead that moment became the first moment I knew fear. It would be the first time I would freeze in response to anger, to make myself invisible and undetectable so that I could survive. This would be the first impression in a pattern created between us that would haunt me for four decades. Before I was even earthside, our dynamic had a hook in me.

Someone was always saying, "I wish I could help; I wish I could be there; I wish I could do something" in response to the disharmonious situation I was in with my mother. But no one did anything. I wished so much for those people to help, to be there, to do something—but they couldn't or wouldn't. So I just got accustomed to doing everything myself, and I stopped getting my hopes up when someone offered to intervene. Self-reliance became my most prominent teacher growing up, and it is why I survived. But it also became one of my most significant roadblocks to receiving and finding more profound connections with others as I got older.

It can be tempting to be needed rather than wanted or accepted. We sometimes abandon our desire for belonging in lieu of feeling useful. But you are enough without your abilities, gifts, and offerings. Trauma, which moves us to participate in relationships operating strictly on give and take, can be sneaky. Trauma shows you that it's protecting you, but it's also preventing you from being open to support. We can be very guarded and not trust others because we have experienced being used and then discarded. A balance is required to have a fulfilling life and relationships, and it begins with trusting yourself. To do this, you must learn how to be on your own side. I cannot stress enough the importance of trusting your intuition and believing in your choices. Yes, we can seek outside help and guidance, but we must be discerning about the sources of that guidance. That's especially true if we have been around narcissists or people who manipulated us and used our abilities for themselves, then discarded us the moment they no longer needed us. Without discernment, we can be a magnet for this kind of person, and sometimes we even become conditioned to look for them, thinking we can recreate the original relationship scenario and change it. There's a popular saying that insanity is doing the same thing and expecting different results. Without recognizing this pattern, it's easy to wind up in the same predicament again and again, and experience the same pain repeatedly.

It took me until I was in my thirties to realize that I was programmed backward. It took me some time to understand and trust my intuition because of how I was raised. I felt like I had grown up in Opposite Land, because what was being said out loud versus what I felt was very different. For example, I would often think that if someone was outwardly being nice to me, they must have ulterior motives, because that's a dynamic that had been used to manipulate me in the past. I thought that if people were being mean to me—cold, shut off, guarded—they cared. It took some time to deprogram myself and rewire my senses and intuitive compass. This is ironic, right? I've been doing readings professionally full-time since 2009. And in the years before I took a hard look at my perception of the world, it was easy for me to see the truth for other people, but when it came to my navigation system, I was still lost. Until I started to see the patterns I was perpetuating and learn to trust myself, I felt like I couldn't trust my own perception of the world. I had to stop caring about what other people thought. That took me some time, though—more than I care to admit, because even though there may have been times I declared that I did not care what other people thought of me, I did care. I would make choices that were not for my betterment but based in the fear of being rejected and lonely.

The more you understand your purpose, the less you care about fitting in, and the less you care about fitting in, the more you know how loneliness can contribute to many people avoiding their purpose. I've never been afraid of being different. I have been terri-fied of being alone. That gave me some drive, but loneliness is deep suffering, and not everyone wants to do that. It's painful when we sacrifice our well-being and our truth for the company of others.

Sometimes when standing at the intersection of existence, which can sometimes feel more like a traffic circle of identities, you'll hear a thousand voices telling you who you are and who you are not. It is imperative to find your footing and connect to all that you are. That is the most empowering and authentic place for yourself. Keep everyone from taking from you what they couldn't wipe out. The more they try to refute your existence, I dare you to emphasize your individuality—every curve, every line—and brighten your colors rather than mute them. Be bolder than ever before.

You are still here for a reason. Even if you don't think you've been on your side, remember that there have been times when you have made choices that proved you were. You're still here, if only to make sure others like you continue. It is not an easy path to take, so I commend you. It is neither gentle nor kind, but despite the efforts of those who would rather see you small or nonexistent, you dare to continue—and I want to remind you that if you want to hide—which is more than okay to do on occasion—even if you try to blend in, you are always going to stand out. Remember that being on your own side can sometimes be lonely, but it does not mean you are alone. These moments will pass, and the more faithful you are to your authentic nature, the easier it is for others who are also standing in their power to find you. I promise.

Tinderbox

MY EARLIEST memories were in our apartment on Knight Street. My brother and I were toddlers then. Adults don't think you remember things at that age, but you do when you are traumatized. My mother's husband, Tony, my brother's father, was a drug dealer and physically abusive. He was always drinking beer in bed and yelling at us to sleep. I remember clear as day the swing he took at my mother, splitting her eyebrow with his fist, even though four decades have passed. She still has the scar. The punch was his response after she told him off for putting us in danger. The day prior, she shoved my brother and me in a closet and told us to hide because she was afraid we would die. I remember holding my brother and wishing to be quiet and invisible until the bad men disappeared. Pretty sure that's where I first learned to disassociate. The only memory I have of living with Tony after that was leaving in a hurry. Tony's most prized possessions were his exotic fish and the cocaine in the fridge. Before we left, my mother made it snow in the fish tank—the next thing I knew, we were gone. I don't remember the time between the old apartment and the new one. I barely remember being adopted by Frank, her new husband. But somewhere between four and five years old, it happened.

The different apartments and, eventually, the home I grew up in were always volatile and chaotic—a revolving door of friends, visitors, and strangers in a constant party-like atmosphere. The smell of cigarettes, beer, and motorcycle grease filled the air, usually accompanied by boisterous laughter or music blasting, either from the stereo or the TV. My mother was always the center of attention, and if you weren't paying attention to her, she would make sure to correct that. Her verbal abuse was a constant reminder of her misery. I grew up thinking this was normal, more or less, but the malignancy of it began to creep into my daily life once I started attending elementary school. She was angry all the time, and the more I began to develop as a person, the less I found I could follow her orders ("make coffee," "wake up the kids," "do the dishes," "go to the store with this note," "get my cigarettes"). The less subservient I was, the meaner she got.

Growing up became almost intolerable. I was convinced she had taken the wrong baby home from the hospital. How could this be my existence? How did I come from this woman? We couldn't be more different. I was seeking an escape, and the idea of death fascinated me. Often I made up elaborate stories of how I would die and what my funeral would be like. I would act these stories out the way I would see them depicted in the daytime soap operas I would watch with my grandmother—over-the-top, full of expressions of regret and remorse from those around me. I fantasized about how my real family would discover my passing, and everyone would mourn me. I felt that if any adult knew how much I pondered these things, they would have me committed to a mental facility. I fantasized about that too. It would have probably been more peaceful than my home environment. My mother would call me Wednesday Addams, simultaneously mocking my grim behavior and brushing off my depression by saying "You're just a morbid kid."

One night after dinner, attempting to silence it all, I grabbed a plastic wrap box and used the razor's edge to slice my wrist. I was eight years old and wanted to die, or at least disappear. Her response was to retaliate in anger and scream in my face, "*You're doing it wrong!* If you were going to do it, at least do it fucking right. *You go up and down!"* After miming the direction and instructions, she threw the box to the ground and quickly picked up her smokes, lit up, and walked away, disgusted.

From an early age, I got accustomed to leaving my body. It became a necessary escape tactic. The verbal abuse was rampant, and my mother's favorite nicknames for me were Cold-Hearted Little Bitch and Ice Princess. This is why teleportation was mandatory for my survival. My only relief was weekends and holidays, which I spent with my grandmother, my mother's mother, who took care of me as an infant and every weekend during my adolescent years.

As I got older and started developing, my mother shifted her tactics, beginning to degrading me in public. I was twelve years old. Puberty was rough enough, as I began developing before my friends. Now I had to contend with my own mother calling me names like Orca and Thunder Thighs.

How do you ever get over this kind of trauma? After years of facing it, it has begun to feel farther away, but those dark thoughts do occasionally creep in. When I started to let people in, they could vibe it, which earned me a sad girl reputation. I attracted a lot of negativity when I was growing up. In retrospect, I think it's all I knew, so I welcomed it. It never occurred to me during those formative years that you could change your lot in life. Even though I had taken many leaps of faith and by chance choices that definitely saved my life, the concept of making your experience in this body different didn't sink in until I was about thirty-six years old.

It's also crucial for you to know that I no longer view myself as a victim. It doesn't mean my mother's behavior didn't hurt me. But I understand her circumstances more now and feel that I understand the bigger picture. As a woman who has accepted her abilities as an empath, I can now see how the eight-year-old girl I was took on the pain and confusion of everyone around her—especially her mother—and claimed it as her own. She mirrored her mother's pain and desire to leave her earthly body. This sadness accumulated like an immense stack of kindling that eventually set alight the bonfire of emotions that I became as an adult. When you finally start to process childhood grief, it can come as a shock. When old anger is ignited, it can be difficult to extinguish its flames. I was so angry for years, and I had no idea why. I hated my mother for so long. To deal with all that pain, I turned it into a weapon, cutting down anyone who presumed to care about me. Becoming an explosion felt safer than being too tender.

It's taken many years to find some sense of peace about the danger my mother put us in, via therapy, recovery, and grief. There comes a point where you must decide if you want the pain you're feeling to dictate your quality of life. I decided that I didn't want my capacity for love to remain based on the actions of another person. Can I ever find a way to forgive her completely? Maybe someday—anything is possible. Selfishly, I hope I can, because resentment is a heavy burden to carry, and holding on to it certainly doesn't move me to greatness. Instead, it anchors me to outdated beliefs that no longer serve me. Until then, I choose to work with this burden. I ask for peace, forgiveness, and help with healing the giant hole in my heart. Or at least I ask for the wisdom to not put garbage expectations or low-vibe relationships into it to fill the void.

INNER CHILD HEALING

If you didn't have an ideal relationship with your parents or guardians, I recommend learning how to reparent yourself. Reparenting empowers you because it enables you to take charge of how you care for yourself and how you would like to be cared for. You can't change the past, but you can change your perspective on it: instead of focusing on what you did not get, it will give you an opportunity to envision a situation in which you received what you needed. It may feel unlikely, but I promise this shift is possible. It won't happen overnight, but reparenting will and can change your life.

Get help with this process if you embark on it. Mother yourself by allowing self-care and proper nourishment of body, mind, and spirit. Father yourself by allowing yourself to receive gifts of love and confidence that come to you with grace. Protect your inner child and give them comfort, encouragement, and support daily. Build an altar for your inner kid. You can use a photo if you have one, or a favorite food or beverage you enjoyed as a kid. Place that on the altar too. Give this child some tenderness by sending it down the timeline. You are the protector of your own heart. Stop the shaming process of wanting to be fixed or healed. If you read this and it resonates with you, you will find more love, balance, harmony, and an all-access pass to love without limits. It can be challenging, but you are supported. Also, if I can do it, so can you!

letter to my former self: timeline healing

Throughout my life, I have made decisions that have changed the course of my experience. I've often wondered how on earth I made those choices. When I was very disconnected from my intuition, I would often do the exact opposite of what it was telling me. I had to learn to trust myself again before I could honor what I was feeling, especially at crucial moments. When I compare my life to, say, a sibling's—a situation in which we had the same upbringing, yet our lives are completely different—I can see how people's experiences can diverge based on their ability to make decisions intuitively. Even though we had the same conditioning, the healing work I did affected my future self because it prompted me to make decisions that I wouldn't have otherwise.

Time traveling by sending healing down the timelines is absolutely possible. There are a few ways to do it. While you cannot change the past completely, you can shift its impact by meeting yourself in the place where you currently are and giving yourself what you need and did not receive in the past. I will share a practice that I found really helpful on more than one occasion. It came to me just before stay-home orders at the beginning of the COVID-19 pandemic in Los Angeles, just before March 16, 2020. It was an especially appropriate opportunity to be uncomfortable and face intense feelings, but I encourage you to do this exercise at any time. All it takes is a letter: that's one of the most effective forms of time travel healing.

Letter writing is one of the most magical and powerful spells I have ever worked with. The art of writing a letter, whether it is to another person when the lines of communication have been cut off or to yourself, has the most amazing capacity to effect change. This is especially true when it comes to letters that connect us to a former self—a younger self, an old identity that we grew out of as we became older, or a past self that we are attached to even though we may need to let it go. We may need to send some energy to these former selves, even if it's just so that they can find forgiveness or acceptance. You can use this exercise for any aspect of yourself that needs healing. Because you can look through the timelines from that further-out perspective, you can heal yourself.

1   To begin, you will need some paper and a pen or pencil. I know we like to use our digital devices these days, but I highly recommend using a writing utensil and actual paper if you are able.

2   Next, I'm inviting you to locate a version of yourself that needs healing. At what ages do you distinctly remember being pained about your identity? When did those moments first come into your awareness? You may have an age or multiple ages that stand out. If you have photos of yourself at any of those ages, great. If you don't, that's okay. If you have some images in your mind or a memory you can pull up for yourself, you can situate that object or photo and assign it to hold the memory or energy, and then put it physically on your altar, or create an altar as a

dedication or a place of honor if you don't already have one set up. Alternatively, you can write your name and age at that time down on a piece of paper and use that. Using your altar as the physical space to do your work, begin creating a connection to your past or younger self.

Before continuing, I want to remind you that this work can be an emotional process. Make sure that you approach it with that in mind, and make sure that you have the time, space, and support to process any emotions that might arise. My recommendation is that you do this when you have an unimpeded window of time to focus on the exercise: that could be a couple of days to a week. This will allow reflection to happen and give you enough time to acknowledge the emotions that move through you, so that you're not tempted to avoid them or stuff them down without fully experiencing them.

3   Once you feel ready, you can drop into your body through your breath. Allow yourself to get very comfortable with being grounded by slowing your exhales and inhales. As you breathe in and out, allow your entire being to relax and your nervous system to feel supported. You can begin this process by deep breathing through your nose and into the belly, fully extending it and then fully releasing it by exhaling slowly out of the nose or mouth. Just make sure your breathing is slow.

4 After a few rounds, it will become time to connect with one of those past selves, or perhaps all of them. As those younger or former versions of yourself appear, I want you, in your mind's eye, to thank them for being present. Thank them for being here for this healing. After sharing your gratitude for their presence, note the ages or identities you saw. There may be versions of yourself that showed up even if they didn't initially come to mind.

5 Now, write these former versions of yourself a letter. If there is more than one, you can write to the youngest first and continue through to the oldest. Or, if this feels over-whelming, choose just one former self to work with first. Using your own words and guided by what you know is right, imagining talking to a friend or a loved one. Show compassion for yourself in a way you may not have had the luxury of receiving. Please give yourself the same care and empathy that you give others but may not offer yourself because a parent, guardian, or authority in your life told you that to do so was selfish. As you write from the per-spective of where you are now, tell your past self about your life now. Tell them who you are today and what you've been up to, and about any notable achievements or moments that would make them feel seen. Share with them any words you wish had been shared with you for encourage-ment back then. What would you say to your former self if you could tell them today what they needed to know about their future? What advice would you give yourself if you could speak to them as a mentor?

6 Next, share a moment of appreciation for what they have taught you. Tell your former self from this perspective what you admire about them, especially if you want to invite that energy back into your present life. Last, I'd like you to send some healing, love, gratitude, and support to that former self down the timeline. Sign this letter, and then put it on your altar.

You can do this exercise as many times as you want, for as many identities, ages, or periods of your life as you see fit. Allow yourself to be tender regarding any feelings that come up. You may have some emotions that want to be expressed or released. On an energetic level, the magic of this process is that you're disconnecting the hook attached to that past self's energy that might be connected to you in an unhealthy way. It's similar to the practice of cord-cutting, but you are not banishing this lifetime or bypassing the experience. Cord-cutting rituals and meditations are a practice used in magic commonly when going through the end of a relationship or job, or even when shedding unhealthy habits. This exercise is also a great tool for releasing any anchors to the past that are potentially restricting you, keeping you stuck in patterns of thinking and acting that limit your appreciation of the present.

This practice has reshaped my perspective and my experience of my past, allowing me to feel empowered by confronting those past moments through a lens of appreciation. I hope this supports you in all your incarnations as you find your way through this journey.

soul retrieval

Soul retrieval is a powerful spiritual practice that helps heal soul loss. Soul loss can occur when we have a trauma, deep pain, or injury. For example, we may experience soul loss if we are in an accident, undergo a serious medical procedure, have a violent encounter, or suddenly lose someone or something we care for deeply, like a familiar, a loved one, or even the ability to do something we once loved. This act of separation occurs between our soul body and our current physical reality, causing stress in both the emotional and physical worlds. Our first experiences with soul loss tend to occur as children—some, unfortunately, younger than you can imagine.

When soul loss happens, we often feel disconnected. We may experience the feeling of being lost, or may feel depressed, find it hard to connect with others, have negative thoughts and low energy, or disassociate. Often there can be a longing feeling, or a persistent need to search for something to fill the void of emptiness. We may feel an inescapable sense that something is missing. More often than not, our response is to fill up on things that never quite satisfy this expectation, and in fact these substitutes can exacerbate our feelings of loneliness and emptiness. In turn, this can leave us reaching for harmful things out of desperation for relief, when in fact what we were searching for all along was ourselves.

The first time I experienced soul retrieval was with a healer who claimed to be a shaman. This is a word that is used loosely these days and gets a lot of eye rolls because it's been misappropriated so many times. However, I believe some people are healers who can legitimately hold space for you in this way, and these healers know how to conduct an ethical soul retrieval. But I digress.

My first soul retrieval session brought back a four-year-old version of me—a piece of myself from that age that shared she was lost and afraid, hiding with other children who felt the same. When the practitioner described this girl, she said she was holding a doll. I recognized this toy instantly: it was my favorite doll as a toddler, one I had lost a long time ago. That doll was a treasured friend who comforted me at that age, when I lived in a violent home. Here's the thing, though: no one, not the shaman or anyone else, told me that this piece of me could leave if it was not cared for or made to feel safe. And leave again she did. It would be another six years before my vulnerable four-year-old self would return.

But when she left, I didn't even know she was gone. That's how disconnected I was from my emotions. Just before I got sober in 2016, there was an intervention, both spiritually and physically. I had a friend pick me up with his buddy and bring me to a lodge to pray

and find support. After hours of prayer, sweat, agony, and visions, I slept hard. The following day, the person conducting the lodge came up to me with a doll similar to the one I lost. She handed it to me and said, "Now, don't lose her this time. You got to keep her safe." I was shocked. Never had I told her about this. Not only did she know, but she also understood that I had lost this child self twice. I vowed that day to take this kind of care and integration more seriously. Simultaneously, I started my journey to recovery.

While I believe you can and should get support from someone adept at and competent in soul retrieval, I also feel it necessary to mention that it's possible to have automatic soul retrieval without someone assisting you. One time I was at a Tori Amos concert, and during her encore, she sang "Take to the Sky." As she was performing, not one but two pieces of my teen self, fifteen and seventeen years old, came flooding back into me. I felt euphoric. Finally, I was becoming whole. Music has the power to do so many things, including retrieval if and when you are open and ready.

You may feel called to do soul retrieval work in your journey. You may even sense the profound presence of your ancestors wanting to guide you to engage in this specific healing work. Science has proven via a study called epigenetics that we inherit not only our ancestors' physical characteristics but also their memories, emotions, and traumas, which adds a whole other layer of disconnection at times. Meaning, you may have a strong connection, emotional response, or reaction to a trauma that you have not firsthand lived through, but your physical body remembers. Your ancestors' memories are coded into your cellular memory, providing you with a survival blueprint. This can feel just as intense at times, and as though you have gone through their experience as well. If you are feeling stuck or overwhelmed by this process, remember that your ancestors are here to help guide you in your healing journey. Connecting to them is also how you create a sustainable way to collaborate through timelines.

So how do we reclaim lost, erased, stolen, hidden, and forgotten soul pieces through lineages? I recommend creating space to do this work when you know you can prioritize getting support via your community and your loved ones, and doing adequate self-care. These are suggestions and not mandatory, but it is important to remember that you, too, deserve to feel held in a container that can nourish you while doing this profound work. I know that it is not always feasible for us, financially, to get the care we need, but there are many empowering solutions available to you on this path.

I remember a time I was doing some deep healing with my ancestors. I asked a few, although not all, of my friends to hold space for me. Please be sure that you are asking those who are emotionally available to offer you support. It is key to ensure they are capable, willing, and have the time in their own life to do this. You would be surprised by the willingness friends express when asked to help. In this case, I asked them to place my image or name on their altars. I asked that they hold me in their prayers to support me during this time of discovery. I even went to a Buddhist monastery near

me and asked if they could pray for me for my healing and protection during the reconnection process over the coming weeks. I
did donate some money, albeit a minimal amount, as an offering of
exchange. A financial donation is not required, nor did they ask for
it, but I wanted to show my appreciation, sincerity, and seriousness.

I did all of these things knowing I didn't have money at the time for a
full-on therapy program, but I knew I needed support. Again, these
are just some examples of what I did that helped me in my process.
There are many different ways to find support that feels aligned with
you. Remember, there is no rush. Lean into it when you are ready.
It may never feel like the right time if you overthink, but your body,
mind, and spirit will know. The nudge will become strong and the
voice inside you asking you to begin will become louder. Your intuition will guide you, and your ancestors can support you. If you open
the door to them, your courage will eventually come up to meet you,
and you will, as they say, feel the fear and do it anyway.

chapter six

MEDIUMSHIP AND THE LIMINAL

I HAVE NEVER MET A MEDIUM WHO said they *wanted* to be able to sense things that aren't here in the three-dimensional physical world. Don't get me wrong. I know that plenty of people want to connect to their intuition. But most people I know who have psychic sensitivity and can communicate with the dead do so reluctantly, or are even made to believe that it is a curse.

In my case, my first experiences as a medium go back to my early childhood. For as long as I can remember, I've had contact with spirits. They were often dismissed as products of my imagination until one day when I walked down to the basement. When I came up, I told my mother, "Grandpa Eddie is in the basement." She looked at me, horrified. She was shocked, as if she had in fact seen a ghost—because my grandfather Eddie was dead. He had died way before I was born, back in 1959, when my mother was just three years old. Neither she nor my grandmother ever spoke of him, so how the hell would I have known about him? Frequently, my mother dismissed my ramblings and sensitivities by saying I was dramatic, rather than an empathetic child with an overactive imagination.

As a kid, I had a rich fantasy life. As early as I learned to write my name, I would use crayons to illustrate images of my friends in the invisible world and tell stories about them. I drew my little space friends and different beings that I would see beyond our galaxy. I know now that some of those friends were spirits around me. Most of the time, the adults thought it was cute, but they were not encouraging.

Back in first grade, when I was six years old, I remember having to do a report on an early figure in history. The teacher gave us a list of names, and I chose to interview George Washington. I decided to conduct an interview with him and asked my adoptive dad to "be" him and play the role of George Washington. More accurately, I needed him to pretend to be him, while I spoke to George Washington's spirit, which I could feel standing beside him. I took this very seriously because I was conducting that interview via mediumship—I knew I was talking to George Washington himself. The adults thought I had an excellent recall for history, or that I did additional research outside of what was taught in the classroom, but I didn't. I now understand that I was channeling.

It didn't take long for me to realize that that kind of imagination suddenly becomes unpopular when you hit a certain age. Around eight years old, I became severely depressed when my imagination started to be seen as something childish—"for babies," as my peers put it. I was never good at fitting in and began to feel a complete discomfort in being in a body. Around that age, I started to mimic the people around me, both adults and the kids at school, so I could fit in. I stopped being so openly sensitive, and I stopped sharing my stories. My home life was also pretty volatile, so I quickly had to start shutting down some of the more frightening things I would see in my environment and mind's eye.

I was petrified of being institutionalized, yet I also sometimes wondered if life would be safer for me there. Flash forward to thirteen years old, when I began having more cathartic and intense visual hallucinations. I began to wonder if I was losing my mind. I thought there was no way anyone could help or fix me, so I did everything I could to shut down those visions, as well as the overwhelm I was experiencing. I used drugs, alcohol, cigarettes, and anything else I could to alleviate the intensity of the experience I was feeling. I also believed very strongly that I would not live past eighteen. It was a thought that would float in and out of my mind like a cloud in the sky. It wasn't entirely new for me to think that during this time: I had been a sickly kid, hospitalized every winter with bronchial issues that started when I was an infant. I had my first near-death experience at six months old—the first of three near-death experiences.

The second happened when I was eighteen years old and overdosed on drugs and alcohol. I remember floating up into a bright light and seeing flashes of memories, which gave me the opportunity to review my life. Then, all of a sudden, I was rudely and abruptly shoved back into my body through my shoulders. I woke up in a hospital, and all of the senses that I had shut down during this time in my life, the feelings that had been locked up and boarded up the way you would put wood on the windows and doors of a house during preparation for a hurricane, all of those protections, were now gone. It felt like all the lights had come back on, like being thrown into the loudest, busiest city you can imagine. Every nerve was exposed and every sound felt like I could touch it.

Interestingly enough, the only relief I could find emerging into the world again was by escaping into astrology and tarot. It was during this time that I found myself learning about the esoteric arts and the occult. I learned how to cast my own natal chart, and teaching myself about the cards helped me find a new path. It wasn't for altruistic reasons, however, but more a desire to find answers to why I felt so different, and perhaps find some relief on some level.

Moving forward over the years, I began to notice how I would try to cover up and suppress the intensity of those feelings. I was fortunate enough to have gotten connected to an artistic and music community where I could express myself. Letting the things going on in my mind and body out into the world wasn't as weird when I did so through a creative channel. Whether it was through visual or performance art, it was a little more accepted. However, I still would not fully accept that I was intuitive or psychic, for fear of being alienated or being seen as out of my mind. I flat-out denied it to myself and others—which led me to alcohol as a means of coping. Tuning things out in this way led to additional consequences that seemed less painful than being alone.

When I drank, I would always black out and not remember what I was doing. In a way, I think it gave me subconscious permission not to take responsibility for what I was experiencing because I wouldn't remember. However, it also opened my body to be a vessel for spirits and other things residing in the liminal: entities, energies, and other beings. I would call this experience "ghost-riding the whip," but it is actually known as being mounted by spirits. This can happen when a soul without a body comes in and borrows yours as a physical vessel so they can come back to the three-dimensional world. Think of it like this: your body is a car, and you are the driver. When a spirit comes in, they become the driver, and you are the passenger. When you black out, you are in the back seat asleep while they are going for a joyride. So, when this happened, I would have no recollection of it. I had no idea that this was a type of mediumship by proxy, which some would call possession. I would do all sorts of things. I would speak differently than I usually did, as if I was someone else, but many people just assumed it was the intoxication taking over.

Understanding what was happening during those formative years would take some time. I know now, after an experience where I was conscious, that it was in fact a form of mediumship. I also know now that those first near-death experiences opened the channel to speak to the dead. But I would only understand that later, when I discovered this ability was inherited—something I did not know at the time.

My first experience when I consciously knew I was channeling was in the spring of 2003. I was invited to participate in a group art exhibition at a gallery in the Ninth Ward of New Orleans. At that time, I was making a series of pirate flags. I would hand sew them for hours while inebriated on alcohol and pills. Those days were often like that. I was drinking and partaking in a Vicodin haze that would allow me to sew for long hours while also remaining social. The process of making flags was cathartic, and it helped still my anxious spirit at the time. It was a way to work out the pain and the confusion of my life that was crumbling by my own hand—through acts of self-destruction, burning bridges instead of creating boundaries, and self-sabotage prompted by imposter syndrome and insecurity. However, I was too self-involved to see my part in what was going on at that time.

Flying into New Orleans, I immediately felt a sense of comfort, like I was returning to a place I'd already known. The streets, alleys, smells, humidity, and heat in the air were all so familiar. Walking through the French Quarter and then to the Ninth Ward, I comfortably made eye contact and small talk with strangers, which is super rare and out of character for me with all my social anxiety. I was in awe that it felt so easy for me to settle in this place. The guest house that I was staying in had a freestanding smaller house situated on the property next to it. This smaller dwelling was formerly servants' quarters, which gave me a sense of unease. The current residents had converted the servants' quarters into an art gallery, which was set to be the location of the exhibition. The house and the grounds were beautiful and haunted. You could feel a shift in the weight of the air as you moved throughout the neighborhood and the property, an almost electric quality. A gigantic ancient oak tree stood in the yard, simultaneously terrifying and beautiful. You could sense what it had witnessed over the years. I nicknamed it the poltergeist tree after the Steven Spielberg movie, because I felt like I could be swallowed up if I got too close to it. Trees are always really loud for me in terms of sensing their energy.

I would find out within an hour of arriving at the place that the former owner, suffering silently from cancer, had taken his own life in the house. Jeffrey, the new house manager, current resident, and gallery owner, and his partner were now running this place and hosting art exhibitions, music shows, weddings, and visiting guests to keep the business going for the former owner's wife. She didn't want to leave the house, but it was too painful to reside there without her partner. With barely a pause after telling me about the former owner's death, Jeffrey shared that there had been a wedding just the night before and that the celebration would continue into the evening before we could begin installing the art show. I had never experienced hearing someone speak about death so casually. I liked it. I enjoyed how it wasn't taboo and wasn't this forbidden thing that people tried to avoid or dismiss.

The rest of the day was filled with wonder and debauchery. In a place so passionate about both living and dying, I felt present in all of my senses. As the night began to wind down, I attempted to relax my nerves by heading to my room in the guesthouse. I climbed into bed and began drawing in my sketchbook to distract my intense imagination—but I kept getting the feeling that people were watching me. In my peripheral vision, I caught glimpses of flickering shadows, but then when I turned to look, nothing was there. As I started to doze off with pad and pencil in hand—a nightly ritual for me—I heard the click of the lamp pull from my bedside table. I was so exhausted that I just passed out, ignoring the fact that I hadn't pulled the string myself to shut it off.

When morning arrived, I bolted upright and immediately yelled "Holy shit!"—realizing that a ghost had, in fact, shut off the lamp. I got dressed and hurried to the kitchen downstairs to find some coffee to treat what was an uncommonly intense hangover. I questioned whether the intoxication was the cause of my reaction, or if it was something more. While making myself a coffee, I started to look around at the cabinets, then began to focus on the state of the sink and the floors. At that moment, I felt a rush of annoyance with the condition of the guesthouse. It wasn't a wreck, but something suddenly didn't sit right with me. Almost without pause, my body picked up a towel and started wiping down the counters and putting cups away while muttering to myself, "This place is just not clean enough. How are they managing?!" I continued puttering around, straightening things, and felt a little more at ease—until a cat wandered in and knocked a knife off the counter. The sound of it hitting the floor startled me. I noticed that suddenly it felt like I was fully present in my body, whereas before I felt like I was moving along with someone else driving. I had experienced that sensation before, but usually while intoxicated, just before blacking out. But I wasn't blacked out. I realized at that moment that it felt like someone was controlling my movements and entering my thoughts. I shook my head and body, let out a big sigh, and thought, *What am I doing? Why on earth do I care?* I grabbed my coffee and headed to the front porch to continue my morning and nurse my hangover.

The gallery owner soon joined me outside for coffee and a chat. I started to share my experience with the light shutting off on its own, and he made a sly remark about how the place was haunted, and someone must have taken a liking to me. Coincidentally, he had invited a psychic medium over that afternoon to read the house and see if any of the inhabitants, including the former owner, wanted to make contact. He mentioned this all very casually, as if it was totally normal—which, at the time, made me feel like a kid arriving at a candy store. I craved contact with the metaphysical world and community. To connect with people, I could finally talk about everything that interested me most: ghosts, magic, and the supernatural.

New Orleans was quickly becoming the subject of my growing fascination, but simultaneously it filled me with more anxiety than I had felt in some time. We hung the art show quickly that morning, which gave us some extra time to explore the city, including some gravesite visiting. Our host took us around and was so knowledge-able about every detail of the places we visited. He even took us to the grave of the legendary Marie Laveau. At that time, I didn't know much about her, but in spite of my superficial level of knowl-edge, I felt entirely compelled to pray to her as I stood on the ground where she had been buried. My body went into autopilot again: I began to speak with her in a familiar way, as though she was standing there with me. When I was done, I offered up the coins in my pocket and took my necklace off and gave it to her as a gesture of thanks for her time.

Soon, it was time to head back. I thanked Laveau and said I'd be back again, not sure about when or how but just knowing it would happen. Back at the gallery, the psychic medium showed up. She was very unassuming and quite ordinary-looking. I wasn't sure what I expected, but I felt very inclined to sit in on her visit. She quickly tuned in and gave our hosts a full report of messages from the former resident. He noted how happy he was that the old quarters had been re-envisioned into something beautiful, and said that he was pleased to see the place in such good and capable hands. She quickly changed her demeanor as she moved her head in a serpentlike fashion and said another spirit was in residence. Her voice became more emphatic and varied in tone, dropping another octave and shifting in cadence. "There is a house servant here," she said, "and she's agitated that you do not keep this place clean enough!" At this moment, it became clear to me, without fully comprehending this message, that the house servant had been in my body that morning. It was also her who I felt watching me, and who shut the light off in my room the night before. The medium then turned to me with a look of acknowledgment and said, "You can feel her, too." I was stunned, excited, and frightened all at once. My immediate impulse was to shun this newfound awareness. I was intrigued and scared, and, at that exact moment, slammed the door on it. Little did I know that just this was just the beginning.

Fast-forward to fifteen years later. I'd been working full-time as a tarot reader and psychic for the previous nine years, and in that time, I created my first two divination decks and started to teach classes about tarot and other metaphysical subjects. I honored the fact that I am psychic and empathic. But I did not fully embrace the idea of being a medium, as I had immense imposter syndrome. This was especially true when I would hear stories about mediums being able to pull names out of thin air and then supply such specific details about them during their sessions. I couldn't do that, so I didn't feel like the title of *medium* was one I was worthy of or had earned.

However, years later, I relapsed on drugs, which led to another near-death experience, and then I fell into a two-year depression after the death of my adoptive dad, Frank. He was killed in an accident and would visit me in dreams, as well as while I was awake. It was such an intense period in my life that a couple of close friends had an intervention, which led to me getting sober. During this time, I started to find my way to ancestral work and wanted to find healing for the previously unknown parts of my lineages. To this day, I credit Frank with helping me on my road to recovery, which in turn led to me finding my birth father, a journey I had just about given up on.

It was as though the spirits brought my biological father into my life. I had been doing ancestor work through magical and spiritual means, as well as through research and scientific methods rooted in genetic testing and various documents like newspaper articles, census reports, and birth and death certificates. After a particular month-long period working on my altar, I received a message that I had a paternal match to explore on one of the genetic sites. It took another month before we spoke, but in our first phone call, he said to me, "I looked you up on the internet, and I saw that you took that gift of ours and turned it into a living." I can't quite describe the shock I felt when, at forty-one years old, I learned that my psychic gifts were inherited. What would have happened had I learned that this came naturally through my father's side of the family? As it turned out, he dabbled with tarot cards himself, and his mother, my grandmother, was, in fact, a tarot reader. She read cards at Woodstock and was a well-known intuitive, and her mother before her was institutionalized during the 1930s after experiencing visions much like mine and identifying herself as a seer.

Suddenly my world started to make sense. It didn't take away the pain of being so widely misunderstood over the years. Nor did it immediately grant me access to seeing these abilities as a blessing. However, it did help me feel less isolated, because suddenly I knew that I was not alone in my experience. It didn't make me automatically feel like I had a family. My biological grandmother still doesn't accept my existence, even though we have much in common. It does assure me that my path, while not common, is not unique, that there is a method to the universe's madness.

Growing into mediumship is just that: it will continue to evolve as I learn about myself. Even without the paperwork, I still have access. It's just like having a piece of technology but without a manual. Do you attempt to figure out how it works? Or do you store it or give it away because you don't know how to operate it? It depends on what you feel is the more significant risk: to know or not to know. Personally, I've always wanted to try rather than not know and feel like I'm missing something. Finding out mediumship runs through my lineages helps me feel less like a phony, but ultimately did not alleviate my imposter syndrome or bring me a sense of fully belonging to the world around me. It did, however, give me more courage to face times of doubt or uncertainty with a sense of ease.

Similarly, having three near-death experiences has given me insight that has allowed me to accept my connection to the liminal. Having visited death is in part why I am more likely to commune with spirits so naturally. Walking in two or more worlds can be more comfortable for some of us, although that can be hard to accept if most people around you are uncomfortable with that idea. It can be very lonely for those of us who live in the liminal. As humans, we are meant to connect with the living while they are here. Yet sometimes, some of us connect as strongly, or even with more intensity, to the beyond. This can feel almost like it's a punishment. If you feel like someone who's had those experiences but is unsure how to talk about it, I want to assure you that you're not alone, even if you don't identify as a medium. While everyone has access to their intuition, I do not think everyone is a medium.

In the same way that some people are good at cooking and have a natural aptitude for it, whereas there are plenty of people who do not, there are some people who find themselves compelled to live at least partially in the beyond and some who feel no pull at all, or sense it rarely. That more and more people are accepting that it is possible to be psychic is a blessing, the ending of a curse. One day everyone will be expected to use their intuition, and this will be seen as a normal part of the human experience. While it might not happen in my existence on this earthly plane, it will likely occur for humanity, and that's enough for me to keep talking about it and proudly call myself a medium from now on.

Protected by Angels, Respected by Demons

W E MET on a staircase. I was going up, and he was coming down. If you are superstitious, you know this was a bad sign. This was the start of my connection to a man I would affectionately call the Thin White Duke. As I made my way up the spiral staircase at a party in Hollywood Hills, I saw him giving a muscled man in his tighty-whities a bump of blow off a ring of keys. He looked me directly in the eyes and, in his English accent, said, "Well, aren't you a lovely bird." I fell for it: hook, line, and sinker. That compliment was an energetic claw that snagged me, his words reverberating through my body.

To give you some backstory, I have been homeless three times in Los Angeles. The longest stretch was three months, and during that time, I began dating the Duke. Our meeting on the stairs was during a party at a well-known music producer's house—it felt like a cinematic Hollywood moment. The music was loud, the house was illuminated with candles and lanterns, and the bar was open for all to partake. After a lot of dancing, I went outside to catch some cooler air. As I lit up a cigarette, lo and behold, there was the mysterious bloke who had drawn me in with his words. He beelined right over and asked me for a light. Chitchat turned into more sustained conversation by the fireplace, where we sat in two chairs that looked like thrones. Our meeting seemed significant, ordained. He told me tales of his success as a writer and a director. My eyes got bigger and rounder. He went on and on, and I was more and more impressed.

However, it didn't take long before I realized he was super high on cocaine and a full-on drug dealer. It became apparent after multiple people approached him more or less as soon as we sat down, interrupting our important conversation to score. But I didn't mind. Whether or not his tall tales of Hollywood success were true, he was the life of the party. He was charming, witty, and entertaining—and after all, he had the drug supply for the whole party tucked in his fancy white suit jacket. He gave me a sample of what he had, and I snorted back into my old teenage ways without hesitation. Gone were my many years of sobriety from drugs.

After several more business transactions and some accompanying small talk, we both agreed it was time to leave. We snuck out of the party. It felt thrilling in the moment, as if we were escaping from our lives. We ran down the dimly lit driveway in the middle of the night, and out into what seemed like limitless possibilities. But the romance of that night, in the end, turned into a full-blown relapse. It was as if I had never taken the fourteen years off to be clean from drugs. I spent three months in a haze, bouncing from couch to couch, living in my car, or spending some nights at the Thin White Duke's swank Hollywood condo. Our relationship was never demanding. We weren't boyfriend and girlfriend. We knew what the fair exchange rate was. He was never affectionate, and I was just fine with that.

Typically, he was cool, calm, and collected—so I was surprised and alarmed when things abruptly changed one morning. After a debaucherous night of binging on alcohol, ecstasy, and coke, we both lay on his bed, staring at the ceiling. As we lay side by side, he replayed the night in words. He reached his hand over to mine, and he turned to me. I was mortified. He was not a hand-holder! And, as he turned to look at me, alarms bells rang out: I saw his face morph into what looked like a demonic entity. This demon was running through him, and I recoiled and gathered my things so quickly I was barely dressed as I made my way out the door. I shouted, "I have to go," and took off without my shoes.

Confused and insulted by my behavior, he followed me to my car to convince me to stay. But I knew I would be gone forever if I took his hand and went back inside. Suddenly, I had tunnel vision: I felt the crashing-down feeling of reality invading every thought and inch of my body, and I knew I had to get out of there. I fled from his place in the hills, feeling doom in my bones.

I barely remember driving but do recall making my way down Franklin Avenue, falling into thoughts of death. I knew I had to end it all. It was the only way to free myself from this hellscape of human existence. I drove off the road and right toward a tree. And, much to my disappointment, I hit something on the curb and my car bounced back into the sidewalk like a cartoon blooper. I landed right back in traffic without missing a beat, as though nothing had happened. I was now screaming at the top of my lungs at the universe, "I can't even kill myself right!"

In a desperate attempt to figure out how to do it properly, I called a friend whose couch I frequented a lot during that time. She went off to work, and I sat with the curtains drawn, screaming at God, asking, "Why do you keep me here? What the fuck is the point? Take me out already—I'm done!" In what felt like only a moment, I could sense an intense energy enveloping the room, and the whole world began to shift inside the house. Before me stood the presence of what appeared to be something like an angel. I thought I must be hallucinating and muttered aloud, "These goddamn drugs. I must be crashing hard." The presence of this being filled the space with a light so bright my eyes could barely open. I felt its wings, large and wide, wrap around me, and then a surge of energy started somewhere below my feet, traveling upward like a warm heat through the center column of my spine and out through the top of my head. I thought, *Finally, finally, it's done. Am I finally dying and leaving this place?* The force of the being was so strong I passed out, feeling as if my head was crowned with fire. I woke up many hours later, half on the floor, draped over an ottoman. The sun had gone down, and it was dark outside. The only sound was the passing of cars, the

coyotes howling, and the glow of an occasional headlight passing through the sliver of a window not covered by the curtain.

I should have felt like death warmed over, but I didn't. I should have felt like I had been in a car wreck, but I didn't. There was something in me that felt more alive than ever. I have physically never felt better in my life. That week, after months of being houseless, I found a room for rent and was hired as a full-time tarot reader in a metaphysical shop. Life was, for some reason, giving me another chance. The battle between living and not wanting to exist on this earthly plane had plagued me before that day, but hasn't troubled me since. And the existence of angels, which was something that seemed like a lovely story but not one rooted in my own experience, became real. While tales of the devil and demons always seemed like an excuse for bad behavior, suddenly it was no longer fiction, although this had me questioning my sanity for some time. Still, it created a sense of gratitude, and a new perspective that anything is possible.

I never spoke to the Duke again, but I've met others like him and his many forms on various occasions, each one a lesson I try to take to heart. Just like our guides and ancestors can be our cheerleaders in times of strife and give us blessings, I always look at the more demonic side of the spiritual plane for a kind of guidance as well. Divine Infernals (which is what I like to call them instead of the more common *devils* or *demons*) are manifestations of your shadow. While often portrayed as bad guys or vampiric monsters, they are an important part of you as well, and when you meet them, they can give you much to consider.

Finding a balance between the light and the dark in life is an important struggle that we must all deal with from the moment we are born until the day we die. Whatever you are afraid of, obsessing over, chasing in circles, or distracted by is not your enemy. The Infernals love to send you down a rabbit hole in search of that which takes your power from you, the thing that most efficiently robs you of your vital spirit. We hear so much about angels and devils, the good and the bad, and the story is usually that angels are inherently good. But while angels are here in times of distress, our Divine Infernals are, in some ways, just as heroic in their efforts.

I have walked in two worlds since my birth. I have had angels stand idly by while demons have come to my aid out of loyalty and respect—we are aligned in wanting to find truth and combat self-righteousness. I like to think of the Divine Infernals as teachers who can sometimes be the biggest assholes in the room. They can be your greatest advocates, because they do not tolerate an inflated sense of pride, and above all, they recognize the good that lies beneath all the bullshit. They like to teach us, like Coyote the trickster, how to laugh at our own antics. They teach us how to free ourselves from self-imposed obsessions and limitations. And while at one time I considered the Thin White Duke a villain in my story, now I think of him as one of my most excellent teachers. In the end, he helped me reach my purpose, and I am grateful for that.

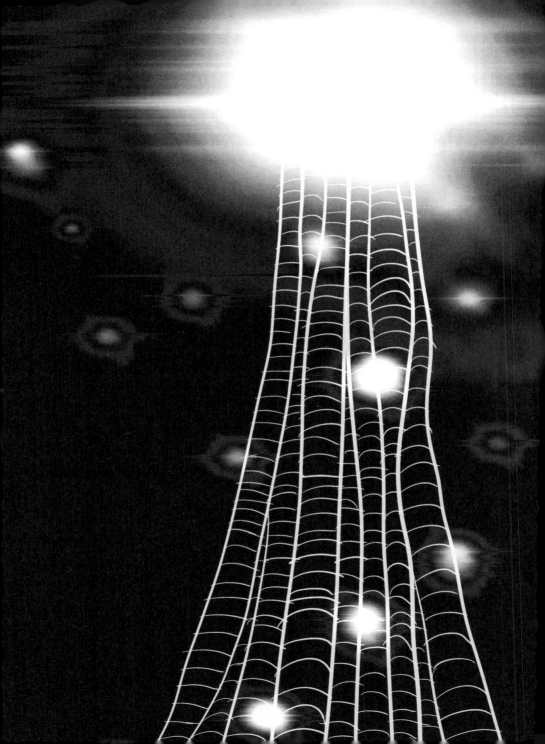

A Forgotten God

L EZA IS a water spirit who is neither here nor there. He is present whenever rain comes, the rivers flood, the oceans reach high tide, or a tear falls, but he is otherwise nowhere to be found in the physical world. Once human, he was so revered that he became a god of thunder and storms. But he wasn't all destruction. Most gods that know how to destroy also learn how to create, and he was the same. Leza wished to help humanity understand the gifts of balance, so he summoned a Sunbird. He gave the bird three gourds and an assignment: take them to the humans. He told the bird that two of the gourds contained seeds that would be beneficial to the humans, so they should open them. However, the third gourd was filled with death, disease, and danger—it was only to be opened in his physical presence on earth, so that he could instruct and protect them. But, as often happens, curiosity got the best of the Sunbird while en route. Interest in the gourds poked at him. His spirit itched with unbearable curiosity. And as a result, he could not help but open the gourds and send forth all of the destructive forces they contained to humanity.

Leza tried to intervene, but once released, even he could not capture and banish these painful things. So humans were forced to fend for themselves. They built shelters to defend themselves from physical danger and developed remedies for the ailments caused by disease, using the seeds carried in the first two gourds. And, as challenging as it was to see the humans suffer, Leza realized that this was an opportunity to provide for the humans in another way. He used this moment in time to remind the humans that suffering is part of the balance of existence. It is so important to appreciate the generosity of nature and the kindness of happiness, because dark times are inevitable. Leza showed the humans how to create through many different art forms. They realized that they could transform their grief into beauty and worship him through these acts.

When Leza finished sharing these lessons with humanity, a huge, glowing spiderweb appeared. Shimmering and translucent in color, it began to take shape high in the sky, then extended down to the earth. Leza used this web to return to his home up in the clouds. Some people who did not want to remain on earth and live with the possibility of suffering attempted to climb up after him to join him there. However, the moment Leza was no longer in view, the web broke, and the humans fell back to earth. In that moment, they fully understood that this, too, was part of Leza's teachings for them, and an extension of his love.

Sadly, many humans have forgotten about Leza and the importance of his teachings. That's why I share this story. He is part of my ancestral lineage, and he comes to me often, asking for acknowledgment and exhorting me to remember those gifts. Remembering Leza means remembering the balance of life: that we will have hard times, but we are also gifted the ability to create art that can heal us. So collect a little water for him the next time it rains, which honors his memory, teachings, and the gifts he's given to all people.

chapter seven

INITIATION

WHAT DO YOU THINK INITIATION IS?
It is not clean and kind, nor is it graceful or blind. It
is a messy and unforgiving invitation to grow yourself. Initiation challenges you to go further than you
have before. Initiation rips you apart, sometimes making you wish you didn't exist... True transformation
requires dismemberment, pulling yourself apart piece
by piece in all dimensions: your physical, emotional,
and mental bodies. As your vessel starts to reunite
with all of the fragments and parts of itself that you

have lost through life, you will experience great joy and bliss. Coming home to oneself while still breathing is the closest to the relief of death without crossing over you will come to meet in this timeline.

The integration will happen over some time. For some, it will be days; for others, it will be weeks. Enlightenment and hope for the future will fill your thoughts, and you will find yourself making plans and aspiring to great things.

However, I want to prepare you for the inevitable grief you will encounter once you realize that, as is commonly said, "your new life will cost you your old one." There may be waves of despair as you try to alchemize your old way of life into your current reality. You will almost certainly fail, and when that happens, you will only feel more confused if you continue to try. You see, you are not and will not ever be the same, so you have to stop doing things the same way.

Not everyone will enjoy this process, not even you at times. It is not your job to make others, or even yourself, understand. It would be best to steer clear from thinking you can take shortcuts or "hack" your initiation your way through this process. Just know that the challenges are temporary, and grinding through it will be worthwhile—even great—if you let yourself accept the possibility of dying and being born over and over again in the same timeline.

Strange Magic

ONCE UPON a time, a young woman named Carmela lived in a faraway place. She was the eldest daughter of nine children and lived on a farm in the province of Benevento, in southern Italy. Her town was revered not only for its delicious food, but also because it was rumored to have mystical healing properties that benefited not just its occupants, but all those who would visit the region. The town was also infamous for having a secret, although not a well-hidden one. It was known for its *segnatori*, or folk healers. *Segnatori* are the protectors of the community and have many gifts, including the ability to remove the *malocchio*, the damaging effects of the evil eye. The evil eye is usually cast onto people out of envy, jealousy, or resentment. Some *segnatori* are also skilled in finding lost objects, healing illnesses and disorders of the

body, and removing fear and worry from the minds of those they treat. Some can even influence and alter the weather, creating favorable conditions for farmers and ensuring a bountiful harvest.

When Carmela came of age, she began the rite of passage that would end in her receiving the full power of her healing abilities, passed down through her matrilineal lineage. While she was happy to inherit these gifts now that she was almost an adult, for a long time, Carmela had resented the idea of the tradition and tried to bargain her way out of it. She saw tradition as a prison, because while she could heal, she would also be seen as having malefic eyes. She felt like it would be a curse on her romantic prospects, as she would be doomed by those who believed these ancient practices were a pact made with the devil, thereby betrothing her to less-than-desirable bachelors of the village for marriage. She also despised the secrecy that comes with this practice. Carmela loathed secrets—to her, they were the source of all humanity's problems. No matter how much she protested what she called archaic standards for women in her family, her own self-sabotaging behavior kept her from proving her theories right.

From a young age, Carmela was taught that she needed to be indispensable to be loved. She knew she would be initiated into the healing traditions when she was old enough, and this would ensure her community's and future generations' health, thereby securing her place in society. While this was important, and Carmela understood the responsibility that came with it, all she wanted was to be loved for being herself: her wit, creativity, sense of humor, and compassionate nature. From an early age, she seemed conditioned to be available during times of crisis and confession. And while she was charismatic, she was not a pretty girl. No one called her *bella* or complimented her style. However, her peers, relatives, and school friends always came to her when they needed advice on how to get whom and what they desired. She learned early on that this ability was something that gave her a unique advantage, making her the person to whom others would confide their secrets and ambitions. This dynamic would often draw romantic interests to her, and in those situations she found it easy to play the role of the cheerleader and supportive girlfriend. Capably, she would build up her partner's confidence but receive no reciprocation. Often these lovers left her once sufficiently buoyed by her help, when they felt they could succeed without her. As her relationships, not just romantic but platonic as well, became more intimate, Carmela would desperately wish for her friends and lovers to see her other qualities. She wasn't just a healer and a confidant. She wanted them to see her bright intelligence, her creativity and imagination, and her ability to tell fascinating stories and to see the possible in the impossible.

Unfortunately, the more she emphasized the qualities not exclusively connected to her future as a *segnatore*, the less her companions seemed interested in spending time with her. Suddenly, they were not available to show support or nurture her dreams, although they had been happy to let her do the same for them. In response, Carmela would withdraw her energy, often confusing her partners and friends. They wondered where their rescuer, confidant, supporter, and healer had gone. Carmela could not understand their confusion until she realized what was happening: they only wanted her connection based on what she could do for them, which left her feeling disregarded, which prompted her to take these abilities off the table, which upset them. Carmela, becoming painfully aware of this dynamic, realized that her only purpose in this life was to continue the traditions of the Janare, so she might as well go through with the initiation.

The Janare are the witches, seers, and healers often demonized by the Catholic Church because of their abilities to see into the invisible. Their abilities often made them the subjects of scrutiny, since they were seen as being in partnership with the devil. There was even a rumor that these witches would gather under their sacred walnut tree to perform dark rituals with Satan himself. In reality, the Janare were skilled and knowledgeable herbalists, midwives, and healers of many ailments. Although Christian rhetoric meant to defame them, they were widely revered. Despite the patriarchal and misogynistic overshadowing throughout the country, the Catholic Church could not eradicate them, and ancient traditions kept their power flowing through strong lineages.

Carmela assumed her role as a direct recipient of this power at the age of eighteen. On the eve before Christmas, she traveled out into the night to learn the prayers, hand gestures, and the history and practices of the Janare. En route, she was overcome with bittersweet feelings for this moment in her life. She had not given up on love, per se, but felt that she needed to put it aside to focus on the responsibility of upholding the magic for future generations. Carmela entered her nonna's home through the front gate, walked into the garden, and then made her way up the stone walkway. Under the moon's light in her fullness, the plants in the garden moved with the wind. The scent of basil and the citrus fruit trees caught her attention as she approached the door. Pushing it open with a gentle creaking, she announced her arrival as she took off her coat and went to the kitchen. The house was dimly illuminated by candlelight, and the faint scent of beeswax filled the air. It was chilly that evening, but as she got closer to the kitchen, the house felt warmer, almost inviting her closer. Looking around the room, Carmela could see the flecks of salt thrown around the floor in nearly a circular fashion, creating a barrier of spiritual protection, and the large bulbs of garlic strung on cords hanging in bunches by the stove. The piles of pots and cast-iron pans arranged in a sculptural fashion cast a shadow of what looked like a bear looming over the knotty kitchen table. Carmela took this as a good sign. She always connected with the energy of the bear and saw it as a nod of approval from her ancestors as she learned her family's gifts. Now, she knew and comprehended the enormity of the blessing and felt the loving support of the generations before her from the beyond, and she will continue to take great pride in honoring this wisdom for the rest of her days.

Kidlat

O NCE UPON a time, not that long ago, there was a boy named Lodi. He was named this by his parents and the whole village where his family resided. Back then, it wasn't just the parents' responsibility to rear a child; the passage through childhood came about through the efforts of an entire community. This support would ensure that all stories, legends, medicine, inventions, magic, and moral guidelines would be shared and passed to future generations. At the same time, it allowed peace to exist by expressing respect for the balance and gifts of the individual when working in harmony together as a society.

Lodi, which in Tagalog loosely means "idol" or someone you look up to, was a hope for his people and future generations. He would feel the pressure to live up to his name even on days when he felt like anything and everything but someone you might look up to. As a young boy, Lodi often took on the role of caretaker and healer, offering words of comfort and sage advice to whoever sought it. The adults were amused by this wise person in a small body and convinced that he would be a great leader someday. He spent most of his childhood with his *lola* and *mga tita*, learning how to make remedies for the sickly visitors that would come to their island in search of miraculous cures. His gifts of diagnosing the ailments of the ill and healing them revealed his destiny as a *mananambal*, a medicine person in the community.

Although Lodi was young, he possessed wisdom beyond his years—so much so that his two sisters, who were jealous of the attention that Lodi received, started a rumor throughout the land that he was not gifted but, in fact, possessed by a demon. They were not just envious of Lodi receiving the attention he did, but they were also frightened of his supernatural gifts and remarkable abilities. They were determined to undermine his path to being a healer. The sisters were convinced by Catholicism, the advancing popular religion in the area brought to them by the Spanish, that healing could only come from God, not a lone boy in the central Visayas.

Not only would his sisters sabotage his herbs and tools, intentionally mixing medicines with poisons, but they would also even go out of their way to tell fearful tales to those who traveled long distances to see him, saying he was responsible for plagues and even ate children. The sisters did not care—not that Lodi was their sibling, nor that his abilities might be real. They only had one focus: to become rich, and to assimilate into the Spanish culture that had so widely taken over the lands. They no longer tattooed their flesh or spoke of ancient gods and goddesses, nor did they want anything to do with the culture of their ancestors. They prayed to a singular god, dressed like the strangers that had come to their lands, and even stayed out of the sun to keep their skin pale to blend in with them. The lighter their skin became, the more their voices changed, the more their hatred for their younger sibling grew.

There comes a time when a boy begins to show signs of coming of age, and he must undergo a rite of passage marking his maturity to the community that raised him. This rite of passage would determine his role among his people, identifying what offerings he had to share. When Lodi's time came, the task he would have to complete was laid out for him: dancing with lightning. He would have to capture the lighting element by being struck by its natural force. This would empower him to give others new life. Dancing with lightning is dangerous, but it's necessary when a hero wants to prove himself to his village. Lodi was no exception, and this was the only way he could ensure his survival, particularly if his sisters once again attempted to push him out of the village.

So came the day when Lodi ventured into the jungle alone with only enough rations for a few days, even though the journey could take longer. What he did know is that he would meet his greatest fears and greatest strengths by nightfall. And while the possibility of meeting an actual demon frightened him, the consequences of his sisters' hatred scared him more.

Setting off into the rainforest did not frighten Lodi. It was relatively peaceful to be among the healing plants and the beauty of the soft earth. He took in the scents of ylang-ylang, pine, and the ripening fruit of the Carabao mango tree. It was just Lodi, nature, and her gifts. He felt a sense of peace, being in the forest. He wished he could communicate this feeling to his sisters. If they knew, perhaps they would understand him, and leave him alone.

This sense of peace accompanied Lodi as he made his way through the forest over the course of the first day and into the evening. That night, he went to sleep peacefully under the canopy of one of the mango trees—only to be awoken by the weight of a massive python, stretching and slithering its long body over his legs and belly. Fortunately for him, he noticed a large lump in its body, indicating it had eaten something quite large and was still digesting, making him a less-than-desirable resource for a meal. Still, the shock of possibly being prey for this massive creature was not something he had anticipated, and he wondered if his sisters had made a deal with the snake to get to him before he captured his new electrical abilities. Lodi remained corpselike and still for what seemed like hours while the thirty-foot-long python continued on its journey, digesting what he could only assume was a warty pig for dinner.

Once the coast was clear, Lodi set out again. Befriending every plant and tree along the way, he spent much of his time in gratitude and awe of the spirit of each plant, rock, animal, and element he encountered. The deeper into the jungle Lodi found himself, the louder the bugs and the cries of birds and monkeys became. The more the air was filled with their noise, the more he worried about the dangers he might encounter: flying foxes, cloud rats, tamaraws, and crocodiles. No sooner was he worried than the sky began to change. It grew rapidly darker, and a mist enveloped the trees. He knew he was getting closer to the *kidlat*, the lightning.

The clouds and rain rolled in. He had been tracking it for a few days before leaving the village. Now he was heading straight into the heart of the storm. Facing the elements, including dangers from animals, was just part of the journey. Now he must submit to being struck by lightning in order to become a man and prove his usefulness to his community. As the world darkened, the sounds began to disappear. The animals were suddenly quiet, and not even a whisper could be heard from the gathering wind. Only Lodi's limbs brushing through the trees and the soft squelching of mud underfoot made any sound at all as he found a clearing by a stream. This was it: this would be the place he would capture *kidlat* and become a living testament of courage.

Lodi sat down by the bank of the stream and prayed that he would survive the initiation. Before he could even pray for his ancestors' protection and the support of the elements around him, his hair began to float away from his head, and his body began to vibrate through his blood and down to the bone. A flash of light streaked across his eyes, and then the sky gods opened up the clouds, and thunder crashed across the land. Lodi's body shuddered and he tumbled to the earth. The black clouds ripped in two above him, and water descended over Lodi and filled the river below. He was stunned, but still alive, now embodied with a gift bestowed upon only the bravest. He had lived to tell the story to those who would come after him, healing the village with the blessings of courage he received that day from the powers of the *kidlat*.

Lodi grew to be an admirable and respected leader and healer in his community, in spite of his sisters' attempts to see him fail. The community decided to banish the sisters from the village for their acts of betrayal against the town healer, leaving them to their own devices and with only each other to rely on. There are rumors that they both were so selfish that they abandoned each other. One sadly lost her life to a warty pig, and the other iron-ically was captured by a Spanish conquistador, who had her burned publicly for witchcraft when she could not heal a wound he endured in battle.

Hearing of his sisters' tragic deaths brought a sense of melancholy to Lodi's heart. He so wished for a time when they could be at peace together as a family. It was in this moment that he also felt immense gratitude for the love and care of his other family members, and of his village community, knowing that even though they may not be blood relatives, they were just as important, and this was indeed his home.

Butterfly Maiden

A S A CHILD, Stella could sniff out trouble more quickly than anyone she knew. In reality, she had a highly developed intuitive ability to quickly assess the world around her, identifying potential dangers with frightening accuracy. It made the adults around her very uncomfortable. Not only that, but she also had a vivid fantasy life: she wove her words and drawings into stories about a world in which there were endless possibilities. This kind of optimism seemed, to her guardians, fundamentally suspect. With any mention of this other world, she would be quickly reprimanded.

She was punished for seeing the truth, punished for imagining a world in which things could be improved. It wasn't fair. Stella often wondered if this existence would ever make sense, or if she was just born to be sad. And she was often sad: obsessed with death, even spending time replaying the circumstances of her own demise over and over again in her head. Would anyone care? Would the adults feel remorse? Would there be anyone to miss her? Her profound sadness followed her throughout her whole life, often creeping out to drag her down and simultaneously piss off relatives, acquaintances, and friends.

The thing was, when she wasn't mired in depression, her natural disposition was bright, fearless, creative, and brave. When encouraged and supported, Stella could create the most imaginative inner world, full of wonder and enthusiasm. However, the turbulent environment she grew up in, filled with verbal abuse, led to low self-esteem and a desperate need for approval. And as she grew older, the only respite for these feelings came through her ability to express herself.

Her need for creative freedom extended to her physical appearance. It seemed that destiny didn't so much call her but rather dragged her through her life over the years, in the same way her astrological natal chart predicted her disposition. It seemed unfair, in her opinion, not to get the option to rewrite her cosmic architecture. So she tried shapeshifting by altering her appearance through modification. From the outside, some would insist that the frequency with which she changed her appearance had something to do with her mental state, that she was lost and trying to find her identity through tattoos, piercings, and hair dye. This assumption couldn't be further from the truth. Stella often felt like an alien dropped off into reality, forced to put on a human costume for a lifetime of nonconsensual Method acting.

For all the fiery independence Stella possessed, she was also quite vulnerable. She grew up in a place where it wasn't safe to be sensitive. To create a sense of safety, she learned to change her appearance in order to shapeshift from the outside in. It started with her hair. Early on, she learned to lighten it to be more approachable and to fit in with the other girls her age. When she became a teenager and needed something more brooding, dark burgundy or blue-black signaled that she was not sweet or friendly. As she reached young adulthood, she adopted various bright colors, like a venomous snake, to state, without words, *I am unpredictable and dangerous if you get too close.*

And when changing hair ceased to have the desired effect, she began arming herself with the magical protection of talismans. One by one, each tattoo was etched into her skin as a blood offering—a patchwork of designs all over her body creating a quilted skin of stories. She often wondered what her memories of the past would be without these images to remind her of where she had been. Could her fate change? Could her destiny be different? The day would come when she learned firsthand that a tattoo could become a doorway and a portal to another world.

Stella awoke to the crash of a garbage can hitting the sidewalk and the screeching of metal from the garbage truck. It was a typical Brooklyn spring morning, cold and muggy at the same time. The garbage truck began its weekly serenade, picking up each can and slamming it back down with absolutely no awareness or interest in what person, animal, or piece of property it was in danger of hitting. It was so early, but the birds had been chirping since three a.m. Everything felt loud: the sun, air, birds, people, smells, cars, buses, and subway were all screaming in some melodramatic opera, and it wasn't even eight a.m. yet. "That's it!" Stella shouted as she took one of her pillows in both hands, placing it over her face to drown out the sound and maybe smother herself to death.

No such luck! She reluctantly dragged herself out of bed to make a pot of coffee and figure out how to beat the day at its own game. She had time off from all of the three jobs she needed to make ends meet, so she planned to blow her paycheck on a butterfly tattoo. The idea to do so was a sort of memento mori meant to remind her that this too would pass, that she should enjoy the moment because death will ultimately come for us all.

After carefully choosing her outfit of the day—she wanted something that screamed "I will hurt you if you come too close"—Stella walked to the subway. But, as she descended to the platform below, she quickly realized that something was different. It was always ten degrees warmer below ground, and the air was musty—nothing new there. So, what was it? She wondered as she looked around. There was no sign of anything different, but the energy felt electric. Stella boarded the train. The subway car was packed with normies going to their nine-to-fives, teens on their way to school, and possibly unhoused individuals trying to make their way through the day. Stella got off the train at the first stop in Manhattan and emerged above ground to walk the rest of the way to her destination. She had a ritual of grabbing an empanada and cocada from the Venezuelan restaurant and going straight to Tompkins Square Park to eat and people-watch.

Killing time there had become a ritual. But today felt different, and she still couldn't figure out why. Once she finished her food, Stella headed to the tattoo shop on St. Mark's Place. She never had an appointment, preferring to play it by ear. That day she met the man who would be helping her out, whom she nicknamed Salty, based on his attitude. She was good at giving people titles. What she didn't know about this guy was that he was actually a warlock, a dedicated practitioner of witchcraft and magick—the kind with a *k*. Little did she know that his tattoo practice was an act of ritual and manifestation, often with immediate—and exemplary—results.

Only a few words were exchanged between them during the two and a half hours it took to get the tattoo. Salty asked a little about why Stella wanted a butterfly, but he inquired most strangely, asking her to share some keywords about how this symbol made her feel. She thought about it and replied, "I want the butterfly because I want to remember that I am free, that I can be colorful, and that beauty is short-lived." As she spoke those words, a feeling came over her, a sense that she wasn't alone, and the electricity she had felt in the subway washed over her entire body. In a way, it was like time had stopped. At that moment, Salty looked Stella in the eye for the first time in her entire visit and said, "And so it is." He made a few more adjustments to the details with his tattoo gun and wiped her freshly inked arm down. The air and slight sting woke her from what felt like a trance. Next thing she knew, she was wrapped up and paying for her new ink. As she was making her way out the door, she said, "Thank you, Salty," as he walked away. Without missing a beat, he said, "Be careful out there," and he disappeared behind the doorway to the back room.

The rest of the day after that was nothing special. Stella grabbed some Chinese food from the takeout place on the corner and headed home for the day. Before long, she was tired enough to go to bed. As her head hit the pillow, she exhaled dramatically and said aloud, "Good riddance to another exhausting day of being a human."

That night Stella had the most beautiful dreams. She felt relaxed for the first time in ages, like she had never felt in her physical body. Her studio apartment was usually drafty and cold unless it was summer, in which case it was sweltering hot. Her bed, usually hard as a rock, would cause her to toss and turn throughout the night. And if the bed didn't keep her up, the sounds from the street below would usually wake her at some point. But that night was so different. There were no outside sounds or disturbances, only peace and tranquility. Her bed was soft and supportive. The temperature was perfect.

Stella was so relaxed that she slept soundly for what felt like twelve hours, until she was awoken suddenly by a sharp pain in her abdomen. It felt like she had been stabbed or crushed, she wasn't sure. She tried to let out a scream, but the strangest thing happened, though. Nothing came out. Throughout the night, she had managed to become so tightly tangled in her bedding that she thought she had accidentally mummified herself in her slumber. As she moved around, trying to free herself from the tangled sheets, it became harder and harder to move. There appeared to be no way out, and she couldn't see because the sheets were tightly wound around her whole body. In a terrifying moment of realization, she knew she was trapped, and panic started to set in. Her mind raced, filled with thoughts of dread as she imagined being suffocated in her bed and not being found because she could not get out nor call for help.

Okay, don't panic, she thought, trying to reassure herself that she would find a way out of this. But then she felt a pain in her abdomen, which became more and more intense, extending through her torso, up to her chest, and then down through her limbs. She was in excruciating physical agony—but her mind was clear. As Stella tried to rationalize what was happening, the pain worsened. She felt nauseated, and she was unable to focus her eyes. Her vision blurred completely, and she could only see soft floods of color and vague impressions of what was happening around her. It was so strange, too, because she realized there was no sound at all at that moment—none of the usual noises of cars, buses, trucks, subway, or the people below. She feared that she was, in fact, dead, and this was some purgatory that she would be stuck in for eternity.

This dizzying experience went on for what felt like hours. Her body felt like it was being pulverized and beaten into a liquid form. Overwhelmed, Stella finally resigned herself to exhaustion. As she felt the light fading, a faint vision of Salty, the warlock tattooist, came to her mind's eye. Then everything went black. As if she was in a sensory deprivation chamber, Stella felt the presence of nothing and everything all at once. What felt like hours suddenly became days and weeks as she floated through the void without form.

The moment her awareness returned, she was back in the corner of her studio apartment. When she looked around, she realized everything appeared much larger than it had before. Her vision, distorted from the pain, made her room stretched and curved as if she was viewing it through a fisheye lens. She moved toward the window to get some air but could not feel her legs. Panicked, she moved without thinking, and realized she was fluttering around with the assistance of two giant wings extending from her back. As the sun began to peek through the window, she caught a glimpse of their gilded edges. She flew to her makeup dresser, a chest of drawers with a beautiful circular mirror. Moving closer to her reflection, Stella was in disbelief. *Where is my reflection?* she wondered. *Am I a ghost?* What she saw in the mirror was a monarch butterfly with gigantic wings that stretched almost to the ceiling. That's when it clicked: she realized she *was* the monarch butterfly.

Was she dead? Maybe she was drugged with some acid or ayahuasca. Even though she didn't do drugs, Stella felt like maybe that was the explanation for what was happening. Not a moment later, a breeze came in through the window by the dresser, sending her across the room. She was swept up by the breeze, which felt like a hurricane gale against the current lightness of her body. Buffeted by the breeze, she couldn't quite plant her feet on the floor, and spent what felt like days struggling to retain balance.

Weary with the effort of maintaining equilibrium in her new form, she began to understand what was happening.

She realized that her time with Salty was a spell, a ritual, and a sacrifice. He had created the portal, and her words became the incarnation. She was no longer human but the manifestation of all she had declared to desire when Salty tattooed her that day. She was now free, colorful, beautiful, and soon to understand a short-lived life experience. She became the caterpillar when she went to sleep that fateful night after getting her tattoo. As she slept, the sheets wrapped around her, forming a protective chrysalis. The painful metamorphosis of her body followed, and now she had become a beautiful butterfly maiden, just as she had wished. And as one of the last generation of monarchs to be born in the year, Stella knew that she now had nine months to appreciate all that was before her—no more, no less. Her final expression of her physical self was the form she had always wished for but could not achieve for herself. Finally, she was free.

chapter eight

EARTH AND THE GALACTIC FAMILIES

HOW DO WE RECONCILE OUR PLACE in this world when we know there are other galaxies besides the one in which we reside? When you know as a profound, resonant truth within your being that there are other forms of life beyond what exists on Earth?

What if I told you I don't believe everyone here is a descendant of only humankind? Or, what if I told you that some people can connect with others outside of humanity to bring us new knowledge and potentially life-preserving resources and information interdimensionally? Sometimes I fear speaking about such things, but I cannot exclude them from this book. I personally have a deep and profound connection to the stars and, dare I say, extraterrestrials—so much so that I have only in recent years become more comfortable sharing my own encounters with them. For that reason, it seems important to include that story and more information about them. So that we may understand the complexity of your identity—the wide-ranging and changing being that you may be and all of the methods of communication that you can investigate to be your most authentic self—I want to give you every option. You may not find a connection to life beyond our life on Earth, and that is okay. Feel free to skip this part if you don't. But if you find yourself a little curious or even intrigued, I invite you to explore the galactic realms.

So here we are. If you've ever felt like you might not entirely be from Earth, you may be right. You may have a lineage, personal or spiritual, that is beyond this galaxy. You may, in fact, be connected to a star being. Star beings have been found in across time and in many different cultures, speaking many different languages. There are stories, legends, and mythologies of indigenous peoples worldwide that contain unmistakable hints of their presence, and encounters with them are still being shared openly today. There are so many thoughts and theories from people who have experienced some form of connection with extraterrestrials. Some people believe that government experiments produced individuals with hybrid alien-human consciousness, which means that, in effect, aliens live on Earth today. Others believe that the first wave of hybrid children were born in the late 1970s as the result of alien interventions meant to save humans from destroying themselves and the planet. Still others insist that aliens are trying to enslave humans. Within the past few years, there has been a sudden interest in starseeds—people who self-identify as aliens or believe they have an alien consciousness. This belief has been very controversial recently because some New Age groups have used this belief to prop up the ideas of the white supremacist agenda, rationalizing that starseeds are a superior race. A note that while the abuse of power in this community is very real, I do not believe that all starseeds and their beliefs are inherently racist. There are many galaxies, and within them are different beings, coexisting in the same way humans, animals, and the natural elements exist together on our planet. Only some are in harmony with us, and they are not always peaceful. And the good news in a broader sense is that more and more people today are waking up to the possibility that they may have lineages connected to extraterrestrial beings and that they can use their intuitive antennae to connect with them.

I identify as an Experiencer. An Experiencer is someone who has been abducted by or made contact with extraterrestrials. While some are not pleasant, others can be peaceful and even revelatory. I do not identify as an abductee because my experiences were not kidnappings, in my opinion. I went willingly and often. How you identify is personal, and you get to determine whether your experiences were positive.

I have listed below some, albeit not all, types of extraterrestrials and galactic families and their traits and connections to humanity. I am not an expert, and these are not scientific facts. They are conclusions from my personal experience, as well as information I have received through my contact experience. As with everything I share, take this information to explore further if it resonates with you. You can leave what does not resonate. I do believe that those residing in the liminal are more susceptible to extraterrestrial, or ET, contact. That does not, however, mean that this will apply to you—feel free to draw your own conclusions.

Arcturians are beings that can be either physical or nonphysical, meaning that they can appear embodied but also exist interdimensionally as an energy form without a body. They are very much connected to emotions and seek to bring more love to humanity. They bring this love in hopes that it will counteract the vampiric frequency that reptilians and even humans with ill intentions have been getting from planet Earth for eons (see page 196). Arcturians communicate telepathically more often than in physical form because their energy is so potent and they are many light-years away. However, they sometimes come here to inspire those who will be great innovators for humanity. They make contact to encourage those people who can create a significant change, sharing not only their love and support but also ancient wisdom that can give special individuals the courage to be pioneers of their time.

If you feel connected to the Arcturians, you may deeply love humans but not be outwardly warm. You could be highly emotional but also reserved and feel that you have a higher purpose to assist in the betterment of humanity. However, the pressure put upon you by this mission can create analysis paralysis, meaning that you might have trouble seeing tasks entirely through for fear of being too "out there." You may feel that you're at risk of being betrayed by those who do not understand you. It is crucial for those connected to Arcturians to find relationships that enable them to maintain their vision and can give them space to imagine a better world.

The Anunnaki were at one time worshipped as deities by the ancient Sumerians, Assyrians, and Babylonians. They were giants, considerably larger than humans by several feet or more. They were highly influential in the technological advancement of man, which is why they were worshipped as gods. Those ancient societies actively believed that the Anunnaki were aliens from a very distant planet called Nibiru. As it was written, the Anunnaki came to Earth with a desire to mine it for gold, a resource they needed for their survival on their home planet. For some reason, the Anunnaki could not do this themselves, so they created, enslaved, and colonized humans to mine the precious metal. They did all this while also gifting those humans the ability to write and understand mathematics. The Anunnaki even gave their human slaves architectural plans to build a society. There are some who believe the Anunnaki will return to try enslaving humanity again to further their mission of keeping their planet alive.

Lyrans are an alien species that hail from the constellation Lyra, which contains the star Vega, the brightest star within it. Lyrans are believed to be connected to the oldest humanoid races in our galaxy, including ties to ancient civilizations like Atlantis and Lemuria. The Lyrans gifted these societies with knowledge and technology, helping them advance. The ancient Egyptians strongly revere Sekhmet, the protector goddess, whose is said to be from Lyra.

If you feel connected to the Lyrans, know that they are deeply passionate, wise, and respected as the original keepers of ancient knowledge. You may feel highly social, although they have a distaste for authority. Those connected to Lyra are excellent leaders. Physically, they could have a feline or avian appearance. They need a lot of sleep to balance overwhelm and must retreat periodically by taking time away from others if they cannot regulate their sleep cycle. While Lyrans like to enjoy life on Earth, they are also here as healers. They have an innate tendency to find the good parts of challenging situations. They are skilled at balancing emotions by honoring the ebbs and flows of life. Someone connected to Lyra needs to balance play with rest—a lot more rest than you may think.

Mantises are insectoid aliens believed to have some authority in the hierarchical structures of interdimensional ETs. They are frequently reported as being present in abduction stories, primarily seen in a role of power. Their appearance is often similar to a giant praying mantis, six to seven feet tall. While audibly sharing clicking sounds with others of their kind, they often use telepathic communication with human abductees. Abductees commonly report that Mantises state that their purpose is to uplift those who protect humanity and the planet Earth. There are often reports of them sharing information with humans, especially with children, using holographic data projections as a means of education. They typically work with and in collaboration with the Grays (see below), but from a position of authority in studying humans.

Grays are who most people envision when they think of aliens. Their social structures are similar to those of humans. Their bodies are slender, with elongated limbs, elliptical heads, large black eyes, and gray or greenish-gray skin. Some are smaller in stature and childlike in size, while others are larger than average humans. They are the most frequently reported extraterrestrials because they are the most physical, although some believe that what we see as their body is actually just the most effective physical form for visits to our atmosphere. The Grays are also the most frequent visitors to Earth.

Pleiadians are humanoid aliens often called Nordic, because they resemble Scandinavians: they are very tall and have a fair complexion. Some say they are related to Lyrans and have come to be friendly and protect Earth's residents. They're highly psychic and seek to connect humans to the stars, as humans are also related to them. There is a long history of humans connecting to them as far back as ancient Egypt. If you are familiar with the Egyptian pantheon, also known as the Neteru, the goddess Seshat was a scribe and the ancient goddess of writing, wisdom, and knowledge. She was, in some stories, a consort of Thoth (Tehuti), or alternately the daughter of Thoth and Ma'at. She wears a crown of seven stars, representing her connection to the cosmos and the Seven Sisters, another name for the star cluster known as the Pleiades.

Sirians are from the star Sirius B within the Sirius star system. Sirius A, the brightest star in our galaxy, is also part of that same star system, which you can find just next to Orion's belt. Some ancient peoples, including the ancient Egyptians, believe they are also connected to this star system. The mother goddess Isis makes her home in Sirius. The Dogon tribe in Burkina Faso and Mali in West Africa have also been widely documented to share a deep and long-standing connection with Sirius. The tribe has vast information based on what they say are their direct encounters with beings from Sirius. They have detailed stories, passed down through the ages, of the Nommos. The Nommos are a group of beings from Sirius who visited them and related detailed information about the stars and planets long before the invention of telescopes and modern technology. It is essential to mention that this tribe was very isolated and lived predominately in caves with little outside contact

with other humans until only about a century ago. Some skeptics speculate that the Dogon tribe encounters with the Nommos are secondhand information, trying to discredit their beliefs, but stories featuring these encounters have been shared through their oral traditions for generations.

Reptilians, sometimes referred to as Draconians, are often depicted as villains. The Anunnaki and Grays are sometimes associated with them due to their humanoid appearance, although the Reptilians also tend to have some reptilelike features. But the Reptilians are unique in that many call them the bullies of the galactic system, due to their aggression and lack of empathy with human issues. I don't believe that all Reptilians are evil, though. While some Reptilians are low-frequency entities running their energy through electronic structures and mind control of consciousness to hijack vital resources, rerouting it for their own purposes, some more ancient Reptilian ancestors are part of Earth's ecosystem and the cosmic order of the universe. Not all Reptilians are demonic parasites. Similar to cryptids and mystical dragons, not all extraterrestrial species are labeled "bad" or "good." In the same way that humans have a wide range of possibilities, so too do different aliens.

Ashtar, also known as Ashtar Sheran, is the name of an extraterrestrial being or group. The name originated with George Van Tassel, an aircraft mechanic, flight inspector, aeronautics engineer, and vocal ufologist. In 1953, he began hosting meditation meetups underneath Giant Rock in Landers, California. During that time, he was contacted by an ET who motivated him to begin constructing something called the Integraton, which was meant to support research into the rejuvenation of the human body, as well as other scientific and spiritual studies. The Ashtar movement, founded around the same time, involved many channelers and healers who began to share psychic messages and teachings from the beings of what they called the Ashtar Command, a sort of galactic law enforcement agency. In reality, the Ashtar have communicated with humans telepathically for some time, stating that they have arrived to create an intervention in the evolution of the human race. The channeled messages received as part of the Ashtar movement and those that have been reported more recently are often the same and state that the command is determined to help humanity avoid destroying the planet with nuclear weapons and thus self-destruction. While I have not personally channeled the Ashtar Command, I have visited the Integratron on several occasions. During my visits to the Integratron, I have had alien contact via telepathic communication, but the name I was given by those beings when they introduced themselves was the Venusians. The messages I have received from them are similar to those of Ashtar Command, however: they want to help humanity find peace and evolution before the destruction of all resources.

On a final note, I believe there is life out there capable of both creation and destruction. We must not consider ourselves so unique that we are the only creatures out there existing.

Praying to the Aliens

EVERY NIGHT Marcie, who is five years old, sleeps in the top bunk of the bed she shares with her little brother, Mikey, in the small apartment they share with their mom and stepdad. Before going to sleep, Marcie covers her whole body, including her head, with the blankets, making sure to hide away from the rest of the world. Every night she visits dreamland. She knows she has arrived when a doorway appears at the foot of her bed, opening a portal that leads her into an illuminated field. Standing there is a child, a kindred spirit, but not a human like her—an alien creature who is her friend.

They are small like her but have pale bluish-gray skin and large glassy black eyes. They play together in this otherworldly place. This world is alive, rich with flowers, trees, grass, birds, animals, and landscapes she has never seen. The colors are unlike any she has witnessed in waking life. They play together nightly like Marcie does during the day with the friends she knows from school: going on adventures, exploring the landscape. They understand each other even though they are not speaking, knowing and sensing each other's energy without words.

Marcie feels closer to this being than anyone in her family or in her waking life. They understand her, and she feels safe here. Every morning when she wakes up, she only looks forward to going back to sleep again to spend time with her friend. They play and find adventure almost every night. They do this so often until one day, they are discovered by two larger beings who are adult aliens. They are much larger than her friend, at least seven feet taller. They introduce themselves as Guardians. Before she knows it, she is swiftly ushered away from her trusted friend. The larger beings motion toward a large vessel in the distance. It appears to be a large silver ship, or what some would call a craft, illuminated with a rainbow of colors flecked in red and gold when the light hits it. Marcie follows them onboard and into a long corridor.

The Guardians take her hand and walk her through this long metallic hallway. She can feel the air change and get thinner, and the taste of metal in her mouth immediately makes her thirsty. While walking down the hall, she begins to notice there are many chambers. There are clear glass doorways and windows to see into the rooms. Inside, there are many beings similar to these large bluish-gray guardians. Each is doing many things, mostly instruction. Some rooms are set up like classrooms, with an instructor projecting holograms of images into thin air like a projector showing a movie. They teach children, who all look to be under the age of ten, about different aliens and star systems and how to use their sensory abilities. Some other rooms are full of beings who look like they are meditating in groups or learning how to heal sickness and injuries. There even is a room that looks similar to a hospital maternity ward full of babies. What look like newborns and tiny infants lie in incubators or in beds, attached to tubes. She doesn't know how she knows this. It's all suddenly there in her mind, like the information has been dropped into her consciousness.

Marcie is ushered farther down the hall, into a room that looks like a lab and has an observation deck above.

As the Guardians bring her in, she notices a long rectangular tub filled with purple liquid. Her eyes begin to scan the room, down from ceiling to the floor as she takes in its enormity. She can see large windows encircling its perimeter, behind which there are other figures, different kinds of beings. They appear much larger than the adult humans she knows. In her mind, Marcie hears them tell her that they are the Knowledge Keepers. As soon as this introduction happens, she begins to see slideshows of memories of her life flash before her eyes. She realizes they are scanning her life through telepathic means. This examination goes on for what feels like hours.

Once satisfied, the Knowledge Keepers start to make room for what appears to be a shift change. A few more figures step onto the observation deck in the room. They are more menacing in appearance. Their heads are large, their fingers are very long, they have dark gray skin, and their eyes are cold and black. As they come in, there is an indecipherable language spoken. Marcie doesn't know what they are saying but knows it has something to do with her. These she will know as the Medical Teams. They do not have empathy like the Guardians or the Knowledge Keepers. They almost appear robotic, moving as though they are controlled by one mind. She sees them making space above the glass for another figure: a large being that looks like an enormous praying mantis stares down at her with what feels like contempt. Marcie suddenly begins to feel fear in her body for the first time and strongly senses that she does not like these Medical Teams. They are not here to make her feel safe or understood.

These more rigid beings come into the room she is in now and are controlled by the praying mantis humanoid. They do the bidding of the one in charge and force Marcie into the vessel filled with the purple liquid. The liquid is warm, like a bath, but not hot. She isn't sure what it is, but they use it to scan her body. Telepathically they tell her that they will make her forget all that she has seen here by injecting her with large needles in the back of her neck. Marcie starts to panic, remembering that she is terrified of medical needles. She squirms, fusses, fights, and resists the Medical Teams. They hold her down to administer the injection. Marcie releases some tears from her eyes. She does not want to forget. She wants to remember the knowledge. She does not want to forget her friend. She does not want to forget the messages and the things she is learning. As they collect her tears, they telepathically tell her she will forget because she knows too much. If she shares too much about them, the humans will not understand and will make them—and Marcie—disappear. Before administering the forgetting, the mantis tells Marcie through images that one day, when she is older, she will be an artist and healer. She will make large-scale paintings one day that are important to evolution. Her paintings will be grids to help bring light and energy balance to Earth and its inhabitants. These images will be portals for peace and will bring healing to humanity and ensure that humanity continues to exist. She will not do this alone but with others who, like her, are being brought on board nightly to learn the importance of future timelines.

The following day Marcie awakes on the kitchen floor, down the hall from her room, far away from the bunk bed she shares with her younger brother, with no memory of the night before. She begins having a series of night terrors full of images of ships and red hot air balloons lowering onto her tiny body, forcing her awake. Each time she abruptly awakes, forgetting where she was the night before. As time goes on and Marcie grows older, her dreams become less vivid, to the point where she can barely remember what happens when she sleeps. Over time, she completely blocks out memories of her time on board the craft and lets go of the tiny being she was friends with. The being who made her feel so accepted and understood is now an adult, operating the very ship that she visited. Many light-years and lifetimes away, he becomes an imaginary friend in her mind.

Many years go by before Marcie will remember and access these memories. When she does, Marcie realizes that her issues of abandonment and the severe depression that enveloped her from when she was eight years old stem directly from her last visit with her otherworldly friends and their disappearance from her nightly dreams. That was the last time she saw them, and unbeknownst to her, she was grieving them all that time.

Marcie grows older, but she never really allows herself to be in a close relationship with any human because she has been waiting for her friend to return. She continues waiting for the alien she fell in love with as a child to find her again and prays that their ship comes back—because she knows that somewhere, somehow, they will hear her call across the galaxy and come back to bring her home to the stars.

chapter nine

BLURRED TIMELINES

AS I MENTIONED IN THE INTRODUC-
tion to this book, we are exploring the tales and stories
spoken in the voice of my ancestors after going into
deep meditation to channel their wisdom and what
they had to share with me in their voice. Blurred timelines are another area where the liminal exists, everywhere and nowhere, simultaneously.

This chapter is dedicated to our past and parallel lives and all of the places and sacred spaces in between. "Ysidro" is a past life story that has haunted me since childhood but came to me only in parts and pieces over the years. The story was complete when I pilgrimaged to Khemet, aka the land of Egypt, in 2022. "Freak Show" is a parallel life I felt deeply and fondly connected to. It was a life I often daydreamed of and wished for as a child. "Two Sisters" is a poem about me and what I thought was an imaginary sibling but turned out to be an actual sibling. I just had not met her until four decades into my existence. And "Before They Were Swans" is my love note to Echo Park Lake in Los Angeles. It was my salvation, safe space, sanctuary, disembodied friend, and home away from home whenever I felt displaced or houseless during my fifteen years in L.A.

Recognize that blurred timelines offer us spaces beyond the immediate three-dimensional physical world and know that we can honor these spaces and places as a reference for our lessons and growth. They are not to be dismissed as pure imagination or fantasy, but perhaps considered as another unchartered territory for your personal growth and healing.

Ysidro

L ONG AGO, in the days of kings and queens, pharaohs, and the great Neteru—the gods—it was an honor to be chosen as a temple priestess of Auset, or Isis, as some of you may know her. The high priests and priestesses were decided at birth. Those who presented favorable astrological and planetary markings were selected to become devotees of the great goddess, the divine mother. So it was in this place that Ysidro, which means "gifts of Isis," was born.

When she was growing up, Ysidro did not connect with her family in the way that some children would, out of fear of it being too hard to let go. She knew from an early age that one day she would leave them forever. She was emotionally isolated, excluded, and not welcomed, so as to keep her detached from creating bonds. She was not allowed to play with the other children, nor did she receive the affection of her mother or father. She often wondered what she had done wrong in this life—never playing, never being loved, and being constantly tasked with cleaning, cooking, and tending to the needs of everyone but herself. Her parents believed that this was the start of her training.

That was until her eighth birthday, the conclusion of her eighth rotation around the sun. This birthday was when the priests would fetch her to begin her journey to her new home at the Temple of Philae. She could not understand her parents' excitement at her leaving. She still did not understand in the middle of the night, when the sky was dark. The priests came, and they took her. She did not cry. She did not fuss. She did not utter a word as she walked away from her home—the only place she had ever known.

She left in the middle of the night and watched her village disappear behind her. She felt numb as she climbed into the boat, where she was bookended by priests: two in front of her and one behind her. There was no one to tell her what was happening. The only sounds were the murmur of voices and the lapping current of the dark Nile waters swiftly pulling them along throughout the night.

She spent many days wondering, wandering, listening, and learning. On one day, it was how to make a medicinal salve, and on another she learned songs of devotion to her now mother, the goddess Auset. As time grew forward and the seasons moved along, as the Nile flooded and receded, she became older and was excellent at everything she tried, a gifted oracle and healer. She understood Heka, the god of medicine, like no other, and became a solid ally to the other young girls arriving each year. She especially took to the ones who were afraid. She began teaching the children, helping them find their gifts.

It was during those days that she began to see him, the son of the pharaoh. They were not far apart in age, and they recognized each other. He desperately wanted to learn what was so intriguing about this temple and about the offerings made to the Neteru, but he was discouraged by his guardians from spending time there. There were a lot of strict rules about this: only some were allowed to enter the temple in order to access the magic there.

As the years went on, the days became nights, nights became weeks, and weeks became years until they were full-grown adults, old enough to rule. The pharaoh's son began coming to Ysidro for lessons, and in secret, she taught him things about magic and about protecting himself from those who would smite him, those who would do anything to take his place, including his family members. Ysidro was different from so many at that time, because she believed everyone should have access to their magic, which is why she would meet with him. However, this would be her downfall. There were spies within the kingdom who made the pharaoh aware of their meetings. The young man pleaded with Ysidro not to let anyone know about their secret meetings in the temple, because the result would be his execution and punishment.

She agreed. But as she was making her way from the market back to the temple, bringing back supplies from a distance, she was knocked unconscious with a blunt object to the back of her head. Her next conscious memory was being at the bottom of a hole, able to see but not move, scream, or shout. Someone had bludgeoned her in the head, but she was incapacitated and poisoned by something causing paralysis, so while alive, she could not ask for help or try to fight for her life. As she lay there, she became struck with the numbness of silence again, just as on the day she left.

As the shovels began scraping and sand dropped like falling rain over her body, she was faced with the reality that her friend, someone she thought loved her, had betrayed her. He did not defend her. And one of the last things she saw before the sand plunged her into darkness was the pharaoh's son looking down at her. She was buried deep in the earth, in the desert, and she knew that she would not be reborn for some time, if ever.

Her soul would be missing or lost in the Duat, the underworld, without appropriate rituals and blessings. This was a mighty curse and dishonor. It wasn't until many years later—centuries—that she would awaken in the chambers of Anubis. He too knew the pain of being rejected, for he had been abandoned by his mother in the desert. Anubis had now been caring for her and safeguarding her body and spirit for centuries. As they emerged from the chambers and stood outside the temple, he said that it was time. He dressed her in linens and anointed her with flowers and oils. He even had a camel waiting for her. And then he said, "You have to go back now, and show them who you are."

Then, with a hug, she was transported back to the land of the living, to Khmet, once her homeland, at the entrance of the temple at Karnak for redemption. Before Ysidro passed through the gates and entered the temple, Anubis placed the crown of Isis on Ysidro's head. She made her way through the temple and to the back chamber, where she placed offerings at the feet of Sekhmet, the protector of the pharaohs.

Remembering the crime she committed, Ysidro fell to her knees, bringing her head to the stone floor of the temple. She broke the laws by sharing the teachings which the pharaoh's son, this she understood. She could not help but also feel immense betrayal that he did not defend her. As she began weeping, out of relief for having escaped the Duat, Sekhmet spoke to her and said, "I do believe the punishment was justified and necessary, but I see it was severe, unnecessarily severe. Please do not worry anymore. Do not concern yourself with the karma or justice of those involved in your punishment, but know that it is done and taken care of. Your retribution is acknowledged, but no longer through pain after spending thousands of years suffering."

Ysidro is now free after thousands of years of redemption. Her punishment will no longer require suffering as the antidote, but in honor of learning the importance of her journey, she will continue to teach children and feed stray cats as an act of gratitude and reward.

Freak Show

VIVIAN GREW up on the road alongside her
parents, who performed in a traveling circus that
made its way across the rough terrain of the United
States between 1931 and 1948. Her parents, a tightrope-
walking duo, were known for their death-defying trapeze
act, which earned them a nationwide reputation. They
performed almost nightly as the Raven and Phoenix,
the Birds of Night, after two mystical birds that knew
no limits. They were often quoted in the press for their
carefree lifestyle and amazing ability, but reporters
generally overlooked Vivian, who had none of the pizzazz
of her parents. How could Vivian shine brighter than her
mother, a phoenix in human form? A reporter once asked
Vivian's mother, "How do you not get scared being way

up high? Don't you get scared of falling?" To which she replied, "Life gets much better when you focus on flying, not falling." This casual way of turning fear into adrenaline nightly was one of her mother's most famous quotes, still cited today by daredevils everywhere.

When the circus family wasn't traveling by vardo wagons in the middle of the night to get to their next destination, they would try to find a safe place to camp and regroup. Even though the public loved their shows and the people of each town loved to be entertained by them, they were only sometimes welcome about town. People would scowl at them or stare with eyes full of disgust, and they most certainly did not want to see the performers out in the day-to-day world. The Norms (as circus folk would call the public) saw them as God's abominations—menaces, pestilences, a stain on everyday society. Yet they had no problem enjoying their acts in the ring. The Norms called the circus members "freaks," as though it was a bad thing. Vivian never saw it that way. In fact, she hated that she looked like a Norm compared to everyone else.

Every member of the circus had to earn their place. Everyone had a unique contribution, role, or abnormality they could monetize. There were Vivian's parents, the Birds of Night. The group of clowns went by numbers—no one really knew their names. There was a bearded woman, a strong man, and a giantess, a seven-foot woman. There were the twins, who were sisters conjoined at the body, as well as the Penguin, a petite man who walked like the bird he was named after, and Olaf the Great, the ringmaster, who was too loud, too angry, and too drunk most of the time to hold a regular job or a relationship. The things that made them not fit into normal society were also what brought in the most attention, ensuring ticket sales, which in turn promised a roof over their heads and food in their bellies. As dehumanizing as it was to be exploited, it was much more important to survive than potentially losing your life to a mob of angry bigots. For every freak, there was always the real threat of four or five Norms that would kill you on the spot for sport and tell everyone you started it.

While every member of the circus had something to market to the public, Vivian was still trying to find her niche. She was getting older and struggling to find what made her unique. By age ten, Vivian spent most of the day learning how to sew and darn costumes. When there was any time between sewing, you could find her running around assisting the different performers with their acts or helping them train or rehearse. Her parents hoped learning other skills would help her discover her own talents. Her parents loved her very much, but because they were so busy with performances, they weren't emotionally available. They had their own problems.

Over time all the members of the circus started calling Vivian the Pigeon, poking fun at her lack of interest in joining her parents' majestic high-flying act. But it wasn't complete lack of interest: Vivian gave everything a go, from feats of strength with the strong man (which proved that she was too small and weak-armed) to knife throwing with the clowns. She didn't particularly enjoy being a target of the latter, balancing things on her head while they threw projectiles at her, but it was fun when she got her turn to wield the blades. Vivian gave everything a shot. She even tried her hand at scrying into a crystal ball since the circus didn't have a fortune teller, but all she could see in its depths were dusty reflections of things she didn't think she had any business seeing. Needless to say, she always found herself back in the same place: hiding among the costumes, needle and thread in hand. Lost among piles of fabric, she spent hours thinking of new and exciting outfits.

Even when you're in a traveling circus, being the only kid can make life dull and lonely. Vivian tried hard to make friends with the adults, but they usually told her to get lost. On one occasion, Clown 3 was in a particularly sour mood. When she wouldn't take his mood as a hint to go somewhere else, he told barked at her to shove off. He sneered, "Don't you have any dolls to play with?" Vivian felt rejected and sad, but as she walked away, it got her thinking. While hurtful, it was true, and just the spark she needed to be inspired. Why didn't she have any dolls? During those hours, she started to develop an interest in making puppets. She began drawing, sewing, building, and crafting her new friends, who would become her companions, the ones she could talk to about anything. The ones who would never reject her or her company. She could have not just tea parties with them, but honest conversations, too. As she created each new puppet, she named it, assigned it a personality, and animated it with strings and dexterity. Her favorite out of the lot was a skeleton. She fashioned him out of felt and pieces of wood. She dressed him like a proper gentleman in a fancy tuxedo with a magnificent top hat. His name came to her the moment he was complete. "From now on," she said, "you are Balthazar, a protector of kings." Balthazar would become her greatest masterpiece and most trusted confidant. She could tell him anything, and he never shooed her away or mocked her ideas. While Vivian spent time with all her creations, it was always Balthazar who had a starring role in the conversations.

One afternoon, Olaf, the ringmaster, discovered what Vivian had been up to over the recent weeks. Always looking for a way to bring in a few customers, Olaf took one look and instantly heard the clanging of coins hitting the admission collection box. The opportunity to capitalize on Vivian, who was now a teen and therefore gainfully employable, was too good to resist. Olaf brought her on board as the newest act of the show. She would bring her puppet companions to life to entertain the masses, and so she did. For the next six months, she appeared night after night. The schedule was exhausting, but the more she performed, the more the audience cheered, and the more people came to the circus to see the charming, intelligent, and quick-witted girl and her puppets.

Every night before she lay down to sleep, Vivian would pray to the Divine and the faery realm that her puppet costars would become human and they could leave these harsh circus conditions and have a normal life. Although tired and restless, Vivian knew that she couldn't quit. Her act was helping support her family, and she also knew it was a way she could be politically proactive. She could tell the truth through her stories, and since it was considered entertainment, there was less fear of retaliation from the authorities. Still, it wasn't her dream to live this way. It was a means to get by. One day she hoped to be free from this place and have some stability and roots in a home where she was loved, even if she was a freak.

Night after night, she brought her creations to life. People in the audience would become deeply invested in the characters. They would cheer, laugh, scream, and cry as they watched the stories unfold. Even if they had heard them all before, the emotion expressed in each performance touched the hearts of all those who watched. Vivian knew she was making a difference, getting the Norms to see the freaks as fully embodied human beings, not just one-dimensional monsters or entertainment. On one particular evening, after performing for a full house, Vivian went outside to catch her breath in the night air. She noticed a shadow making its way through the tent, the silhouette of a woman she did not recognize. As the shadow emerged from the tent and made its way outside, it called her name. "Good evening, Vivian. My name is Sheri. I've heard all about you through the winds over these lands. I have a proposition for you." Vivian's ears perked up at the last part of Sheri's message.

"Would you like to be free of this place?" Sheri continued. "What if I make your puppets famous? Would you accept my offer?" Vivian desperately wanted out of the circus. Even though she performed to full houses every night, Olaf never let her see a dime from the ticket sales. Her parents became increasingly distant, and she had to brave the wrath of authority should she protest performing for a night. Then a mysterious stranger just happened to appear with a way out—a way for Vivian and her brood of puppets to be free and live a normal life. It also happened to be a full moon eclipse that evening. The omens for change were written in the sky that evening. In haste and without asking if there were conditions, Vivian thought, *I've got nothing to lose*, and shouted *"Yes!"* Without a moment to spare, Sheri began to recite an incantation in another tongue, one unfamiliar to Vivian—or anyone else, for that matter.

There was no radical change or sudden eruption of thunder and lightning. In fact, there was a quiet that Vivian had never experienced before. As she looked out into the night landscape with hope, the eclipse began, and it was suddenly too dark to see the horizon. Vivian was entranced with the natural world's magic, and Sheri's words had revived her spirit. As she felt the shift in the air, she turned around to follow up with Sheri about what she would need in exchange, but just like the moon, Sheri had disappeared. It was like she had evaporated into the night sky.

Vivian went to sleep that evening with a sense of relief. She gathered up her puppets and brought them to her vardo to ensure they got their rest from the day, too. Before retiring to bed, Vivian pulled out a large pair of scissors from her sewing supplies. She wanted to refresh the strings on Balthazar. As she carefully cut the puppet strings from his limbs and head, she felt an enormous sense of gratitude. Her eyes began to pool with water as she felt so much love for her most trusted companion. Placing him carefully back on the shelf with the others, Vivian wondered if Sheri, the magical stranger, had been real, and if all that freedom she promised in making her puppets famous wasn't just something she had made up.

The following day, the sound of roosters and the sun's brightness shined through the vardo's wooden-slatted shade. The sun brightly illuminated a corner of the wagon. Vivian slowly opened one eye to stare at the ray of light, watching the dust particles move like fairies dancing in the wind. She sat upright, raised her arms, and looked around the room, muttering, "Well, we are all still here." No sooner did she speak than she saw all of her companions were still there—except for Balthazar. He was gone—nowhere to be found. She looked up and down and right and left, under the bed and in every nook and cranny. He was gone. In a panic, Vivian leaped outside her wagon in her cotton nightdress. Everyone was gone. The tents, the freaks, the animals, the mysterious stranger, and her precious Balthazar were gone. There was no noise, only the rustling of a sound with the wind. There was a note pinned to the door of her vardo by the sharp blade of a throwing knife. It simply said, "Gone Fishing." There was no one. Vivian had gotten her freedom—but at what cost?

Several months passed. Vivian managed to secure a room for rent and employment at a nearby town's dry-cleaning business. It was a promising job for a girl with no roots. She even picked up extra money on the side, offering alterations to the fashionable men and women in the city. She often cried herself to sleep nightly, confused by the whole circumstance. She was wondering what had happened to her parents and her beloved Balthazar. How could they abandon her? Nothing made sense. Technology was advancing. People wanted to go to the movies, not the circus. So how had the show in which she'd grown up simply moved past her and left her here?

After several years, Vivian would begin to reconcile the past by pretending it never happened. She started to fit in with the Norms, pretending she was one of them. She made up stories of her parents' deaths, saying that she was an orphan from another town several states away.

It made life so much simpler. She continued working at the dry cleaner and was such a good employee that they gave her a raise and even the title of head laundress. Her life wasn't dramatic—it was ordinary, and that was just fine. Vivian was predictable, and every day she would post up in front of the TV to watch her shows while she worked. This pastime was how she became knowl-edgeable about modern culture, music, and the product advertisements of the day.

One day just like any other, when nothing special seemed to be happening, she sat down for her show. When the music started, the upbeat tempo caught her attention. It sounded familiar, somehow. The camera panned around to the backing band, which she imme-diately recognized as some of the clowns she had grown up with (without makeup, of course). She could not believe her eyes, and then it happened. There he was. It was Balthazar. Her Balthazar singing and dancing on the screen. He was alive! Then it hit her: he was famous, and she was free. The prayers she made and the promise Sheri shared had come true, but not in the way Vivian had imagined. As she stood in awe with her jaw prac-tically on the floor and a twinge of heartbreak in her chest, a regular customer of the dry-cleaning business busted through the front door, sending the bells on it ringing, and shouted to a passerby, "Be careful what you wish for!" Vivian replied, "No kidding," and went back to work. She felt a pang of regret and remorse for not being alongside Balthazar and his newfound success. At the same time, she did genuinely miss her parents and her former companion. She did not forget the chaotic nature of her life in the circus and the constant fear for her life precipitated by those determined to demonize or misunderstand her and her fellow travelers. The sacrifice of those dear relationships for a life of stable consistency gave her peace of mind that she believed made it all worth it.

Two Sisters

Two sisters:
One was black,
One was white.
One was wrong,
One was right.
How in this world did they become a pair?
How in this world would this ever be fair?

Two sisters:
One filled with love,
One filled with hate.
One wished to be pious,
One wanted to be great.
Why on earth would Creator invent fears?
Why on earth would Creator allow tears?

And as above,
We find the same below.
Two sisters born
Of the same rainbow.

For without one,
There cannot be the other.
Without balance,
There is no way to discover
The laws of nature
And balance of peace,
The harmony of opposites
And wonders that never cease.

Before They Were Swans

I MISS THE way you were: dirty, dusty, with a faint hint of sparkle when the sun hit you just right in the early morning. Gleaming like you still had a little promise of hope to greet the day. The water below reflects a murky vision of you. The turtles are the same, still thriving and resilient—red-eared sliders without a care in the world. Rusty petals and a faint smell of stagnant waters. Blue herons, red-tailed hawks, and the occasional cormorant basking in the sun. Every year a new promise of beauty, even if short lived. You proved them wrong by exhibiting the most beautiful lotus blooms.

I knew you were getting tired when they became less and less numerous. You possessed grace even when exhausted by the wrong conditions. Not enough people appreciated you. When they moved the Lady,

your guardian, I often wondered if it changed the feng shui of the land. All these new folks started appearing. You grew up so fast when the new neighbors arrived. It wasn't a few years before I barely recognized the faces that had been so familiar. The faint smell of eucalyptus, urine, and fuel remained, but you looked different. You felt different. Where did your spirit go? You called your children home to you for a time and did what you could, but things would change again.

I remember spending countless nights visiting you and running to you for comfort, to be held by your embrace. I will never forget the way you held me when I needed safety. Floating atop your waters, pedaling like my life depended on it, flask in hand, or sleeping in my car parked on the side of the road to wake up to your fountain cascading, cleansing my weary spirit of fear. Loving me whether I smoked or not. Today is different. You still love me, but not how a fierce mother would, but more like a grandmother watching her loved ones from a distance. With hindsight, wisdom, and great stories to tell. Knowing it will all be gone soon. I tell you, I remember you, and I remember those boats before they were swans.

chapter ten

UNMASKING

IN 2019, I WAS DELIGHTED TO FIND
out that I was neurodivergent and autistic. It finally felt
like the world made sense. For years I had wondered if I
was born broken. I wasn't sure why I was the way I was.
It couldn't just be me being psychic, or highly empathic.
There were so many things that I had no explanation
for that caused me a lot of distress and pain over the
years. Yet there was nothing visibly wrong with me. So,
on the wise hunch of a friend, I started to search for
answers that might help it all make sense. This friend

has become like a sibling to me over the years and has seen me through both good fortune and bad. She has an autistic son that I bonded with immediately upon meeting him. Once, during a tough time in my life, she said, "I suspect maybe you are on the spectrum." Based on the ways I would react to overstimulation, including my tendency to have meltdowns due to stress, she identified my behaviors with her son's. This sent me on a journey of questioning if I was, in fact, on the spectrum.

I researched all I could find about autism in women. There's not much information for adults, let alone when it comes to feminine perspective about autism. Most studies have been about boys, and stereotypes suggest character traits like being cold and unfeeling, or good at mathematics. Stereotypes like that speak to only a small percentage of those on the spectrum. This kind of narrow range of study leads to autistic people being represented in a very specific way in movies and on TV. Usually, we see boys or men with a hyperintellectual interest in mathematics and science who present a cold and unemotional demeanor. But that doesn't cover so many of the people who are on the spectrum. For example, while I enjoy science and technology, I'm not a fan of math, and I'm not without emotion. In fact, I have an overabundance that I don't know how to regulate at times.

Down the rabbit hole I went, looking for answers. When I finally found them, it was in the stories of other women. Like a lightbulb flicking on, I suddenly heard myself through their voices. I started crying in recognition.

The strength of all of this new information was hitting me even harder than it normally might have, because it was a very emotional time for me: I had been sober for just three years and finally felt ready to face some of the discomforts I was feeling about existing in a body. It wasn't just the emotional pain that needled me, but even minor physical aches and other sensory things that wouldn't usually bother people. For some reason, I could not help but be overstimulated at all times.

I had to fight repeatedly with my insurance and my doctors to get diagnosis and treatment. Learning to advocate for myself with people who did not take me seriously was mentally and physically exhausting. Most places don't want to see you if you're an adult. They wonder what your motive is. Some places barely listened, taking one look at me before telling me I have complex post-traumatic stress disorder, or C-PTSD. I do have C-PTSD. But I think a lot of the post-traumatic stress disorder I have comes from being on the spectrum and not being able to regulate or give myself appropriate care when challenges come up and I need support. After several months of going back and forth with my insurance, I finally found a doctor who would reluctantly listen to me and proceeded to tell me that, yes, in fact, I was on the spectrum.

To this day, getting an autism diagnosis is extremely challenging. It's like you have to know somebody, be a child, or exhibit outward displays of needing a lot of support in day-to-day functioning. I identify as having minimal support needs, which means

I do not have a caregiver or need an aide daily. I do many things independently, but it's still challenging sometimes to get support.

But in the end, it was worth it: finding out I was on the spectrum was magical. I don't know how to describe it other than it finally felt like I had this missing piece to a puzzle that I've been unable to complete my whole life. It haunted me day and night to know something was missing, but I could not describe what I was looking for. Suddenly, here I was with information in hand, finally understanding what was happening all these years and why. To know how I processed situations and to be able to see that some of my skills—such as my ability to create and to focus deeply on something interesting to me—were more of my autistic traits was such a gift.

And yet, as it often is after we feel ecstatic, I immediately felt the crash and burn of a comedown. I started to become painfully aware of all the times in my life when my caregivers, my peers, or previous romantic partners could not support me. It left me agonizing, wondering what would have happened in my life had I received proper care. Would living have been less complicated? Would it have made a difference when I was misunderstood, called difficult, or put in harm's way? I have so often wandered into painful and dangerous situations because I wasn't able to read the room. By missing subtext, subtle social cues, or people around me being dishonest, I've inadvertently put myself in harm's way. I mean, even down to early sexual experiences, and finding intimate connection so painful, my life has been so much more difficult without that ability. During those times, I thought that if this was all sex and love was, I didn't want it, and shut myself down. Relationships were scary and not to be trusted, so what if I could have navigated them more easily, just like everyone else seemed to be able to do?

So began a lengthy period of grief and depression. I'm not sad I came to this realization. I'm not. I'm grateful that I had to learn how to rebuild connection from a trustworthy place, to know now how to give myself the support I need. It's still a work in progress, but most of the time, I've stopped apologizing for requiring safety to feel supported.

Some people ask me if being autistic has made me psychic. I still need more time to reflect on how those two things are related, as it's all still new to identify this way. I don't think they exist because of each other—but I tend to think of my autism as my operating system and the psychic stuff as the internet browser that connects me to the world, if that makes sense. While I am highly intuitive and can know many things or find out many things for other people who come to me for readings, I'm still human. Sometimes when I'm not sure about something that is happening or being said, and I feel that my autistic way of processing is preventing me from "getting" some kind of subtle distinction or nuance, I have to check in with people I love and care about, and trust them to give me direct connection and feedback. I have to ask about things that most regular allistic (neurotypical) people know, because quite honestly I don't. It's taken some time to forgive myself for times when I betrayed my instinct and inner knowing. That's always something that's going to come up when you are finding your way back to a space that is healing for you. Forgiving self-betrayals will be a recurring theme as you unmask.

For those of you who have traveled the same path and realized that you are on the spectrum, what comes next? You'll want to work on rediscovering yourself by figuring out who you are without the mask. Who are you when you are not catering to someone else's comfort? Rediscovering yourself can be painful, but I encourage you to return to the things that bring you joy and pleasure. If it brings you joy to spend hours figuring out a puzzle or learning about something that makes you happy, do it. In these years that I've been learning to rediscover myself, I found that I have a strong love for and connection to reptiles, which is something that I was never allowed to explore when I was younger because my family didn't believe this interest was for girls. As I get older, I've explored these kinds of interests and committed myself to being curious about the things I once worried would make me stand out too much. I've trained myself to not see those things as negative or positive. When you're unmasking, find ways to stop pretending to be someone else—find ways to be your authentic self, even if someone once discouraged you from exploring them.

The lifelong experience of residing in a liminal space can help you connect the dots if you are going through the process of rediscovery. The spectrum, after all, is just that: there's no starting or ending point, nothing that's broken, and nothing that needs to be fixed. The only thing that has to happen if you are on a spectrum is that you must learn how to exist in those spaces and give yourself the proper support you need to continue to flourish in your life's journey.

I summon my courage, and release the lies.
I call back my power, and let my spirits rise.
I call back my wisdom.
I call back the night.
I call back my power, that is my right!

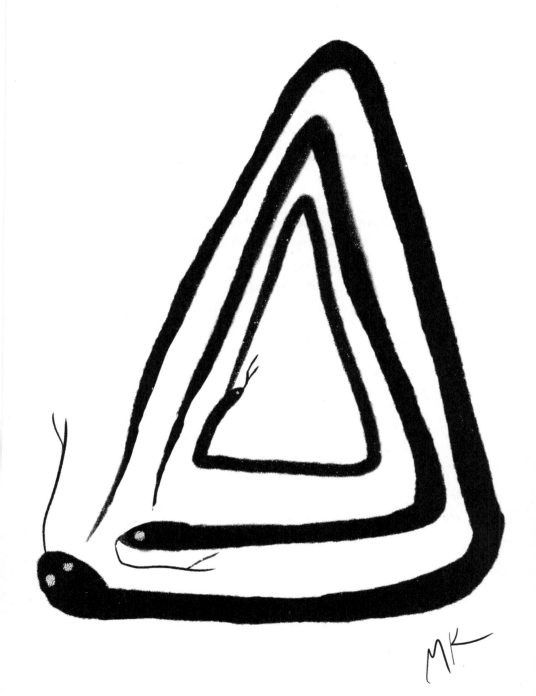

chapter eleven

HOLY OF
THE HOLIES

AS I LEANED INTO THE SHOWER
curtain, reenacting a visit to the Tabernacle, I pushed
my face and body into the fabric until I found myself
inside the tub. Leaning in, placing my face between
the faucets, I pretended they were the two angels
atop the Ark of the Covenant. I whispered, "Are
you there, God? It's me, Marcella," and turned the

faucet settings to hot. As the water began to flow, a voice like that of Lurch from *The Addams Family*, low and deep, spoke back: "You rang?" I laughed aloud.

My connection to the Creator, God, the Universe, the Divine, or whatever you like to call Spirit has always entertained a sense of humor. Perhaps it's because it's the only connection, aside from my relationship to my creativity, that I've never felt a disconnect from or felt a blockage to. That doesn't mean I don't get creative blocks, or that it's a perfect relationship and we don't have problems. I've spent my whole life seeking and seeing the horrors in most things. At the same time, I was looking for peace and the sacred and finding it in the most unexpected places.

I was a melancholy kid. The teacher would call my name in the second grade, and I would throw my head over my folded arms on the desk, flipping my waist-length hair over me to hide myself completely. I hid because the immediate assumption when someone yelled my name was that I was in trouble. My mother constantly screamed, threw things, and said vile things to us, her children. She often called me Wednesday Addams, Sarah Bernhardt, or "cold-hearted little bitch," because I was so sullen. If I weren't thinking about my funeral or crying, I would be mentally evacuating my body, which I now know is disassociating. It was a challenging environment to grow up in, and I could not understand how I ended up there, but I digress. This chapter isn't about my mother or lack of parental support for my big feelings.

I tried to have friends when I was a kid, but it was hard. I mean, it's still a challenge as an adult, and I'm often still filled with intense emotions that most people are uncomfortable with. With trauma comes humor, though, and that usually is relatable. Growing up, I had a few homes, but the place I spent most of my childhood was chaotic. It was a revolving door of visitors, illegal activities, and sinister vibes. I shared a room with my youngest sibling, my sister, who was five years younger than me, until I was thirteen. I had no privacy or quiet spaces to hide, so often, I would walk myself to the Catholic church up the street. The smell of the incense, the flickering of the candles, and the quiet made me feel safe. I could think and hear my thoughts in this place. I could feel held and supported. As I got older, I would invite myself or ask if I could visit my school peers of other faiths' homes. I would inquire if I could go to their houses, churches, temples, and places of worship. I would even attend a neighborhood friend's Bible study with her family. She was never allowed to come to my house, though, because my house was known as "the party house full of heathens." My school friend and her family, who were Jehovah's Witnesses, came to the door one weekend. They came to spread the word of God and asked my family about finding God and giving up their sinful ways. I remember being mortified because my adoptive dad answered the door hungover, looking like a disheveled biker Jesus, and essentially told them to fuck off, then slammed the door in their faces. I was never allowed at that girl's house again, and she would barely look at me at school anymore after that happened.

Often when I felt alone, I would turn to my art or to speaking to the Divine. I would find a connection, and things would feel okay. The ghosts and spirits that surrounded me, whether in the ether or as the embodiment of animals in nature, never disappointed me. I would channel their words in my poems and songs and draw their faces. The trees were always confidants in my ever-changing social circles. I would always find one tree friend to commune with within the area or neighborhood I lived in.

I often moved around quite a bit as a kid, living between my mother's and grandmother's apartments. As a young adult I would find myself moving into a new apartment every six months. It felt like I needed to change my location frequently to reflect the changes happening *to* me.

Keeping friends is also challenging when you are so open and sensitive. It's not anyone's fault, but I have come to realize that being a Seer and walking a path of a priestess is a lonely fucking place. Most people don't get it. They want you to be in their life, but on their conditions, and that's something I've never been able to do, at least not for a long time. I could mask my nature and play a role for a time. I think that's because, being autistic, I learned how to hide by mimicking and parroting the people around me to fit in. But I could never keep it up for long enough. Eventually, the mask would crack, the act would crumble, and I would fold and become myself again. I found that most people did not like the sensitive being I was. I have this uncanny ability to pinpoint hurt in someone, and while it's not intentional, I often made observations that wounded them or lashed out with a sharp tongue that sliced into their greatest vulnerabilities. This tendency could make the experience of human-ing very challenging. I knew my words could cut people down, and that I was especially prone to do so when angered, so I just stopped communicating for a long time. Learning how to create healthy boundaries and articulate my feelings before exploding would take years. It's something I'm still learning how to navigate, with support.

But regardless of my follies when it comes to human relations, I can always return to my connection to the Divine and feel a sense of belonging there. The one time in my life that I did not feel a connection to the Divine was in the last six months of my use and abuse of alcohol and pills. When Frank, my adoptive dad, died in 2014, I was going through a breakup with someone on whom I projected a lot of unrealistic expectations and rescuing ideas. This dynamic went both ways: we each thought the other could save us from ourselves. That wasn't possible or true. And when Frank passed unexpectedly, the fantasy bubble of this relationship burst abruptly. A distracted driver took Frank's life in a motorcycle accident. I was heartbroken and crushed. Frank was the only supportive masculine figure in my life. He adopted me when I was five and loved me unconditionally. Even though we weren't in constant contact since he divorced my mother and I moved to California, we always felt connected. I wasn't his child by blood, but I was his kid, the only one capable of helping his brothers get his affairs in order, arranging the funeral, and dealing with the legalities of his passing.

When you go through these heavy experiences, you quickly experience another type of loss when you realize that there are those around you who can't cope. My ex and I broke up, there was no support for me during this time, and I fell heavily into a two-year bottom. I was waking up, drinking coffee, and taking legal amphetamines (diet pills) to wake up and go to work. I would come home, drink beer and mezcal, and take Klonopin until the sun went down to pass out eventually. Then I would wake up and do it all over again, like some Groundhog Day purgatory. Still, this whole time I was working, doing readings. It's no wonder that, at the time, so many of the people I saw were in messy emotional situations. I think you pull in clients who reflect your emotional state, so if you're working through something, others who are in similar places will find you.

This downward spiral lasted almost two years. During that time, my life and personal essence were slowly getting dimmer and darker. Then one day, I noticed a feeling in me, almost like a pilot light going out: my connection to the Divine was no longer there. It suddenly felt so quiet inside my head. I felt like I was yelling into a void, like a single-sided game of Marco Polo. Nobody could hear me, and there was no response to my questions. I was truly alone. I couldn't create. I just got more and more depressed and more and more isolated. I vacillated between pushing people away or making limp attempts to seek help. Still, many of the relationships around me at that time were very much at a distance, and I think I intentionally, if subconsciously, had made them that way. I wanted, on some level, to be surrounded by people who weren't available, people who wouldn't call me out on my bullshit, or people who were just so self-involved that they didn't really know what was happening in my life. I would distance myself and hide daily in my using.

I was spiraling out and didn't know how to continue, but I was running on the fumes of my life force energy at this point. Getting back into a life connected to the Divine and things that brought joy, I felt, would take a miracle. By the way, I do believe in miracles, and that sometimes Spirit works through certain people. Those miracles can come in the form of many things—usually, it's a word, an action, or someone stepping in to help. I found this kind of intervention in a friend and his buddy who reached out to me to say they were going to a sweat lodge for a ceremony. They were driving through town and thought I should come, and they said they could pick me up soon. I was desperate for relief, so I said yes and packed up my stuff. We drove up from Los Angeles to central California, where we entered the house of a woman who was dear friends with my buddy. She is an Apache woman and a respected healer in her community. After some hours of preparation and catching up, we sweat, prayed, cried, and laughed together. In that place, I lay on the floor and felt the cold earth on my face. For the first time in what felt like a year, I heard Creator. I heard Spirit. The stars suddenly became visible. It was like the ceiling of the lodge opened up, and all I could see was the galaxy.

The stars are often the only thing that calms me. There was a feeling of being on a direct line to something greater than myself, and as I sweat, I purged so much out of me. I felt all of the despair of the past two years leaving me and saw pieces of my own spirit coming back down through the lodge. The fragments of my soul and broken, lost pieces of my spirit all returned to my body. We spent the night talking for hours and thanking our ancestors. Before I passed out, I changed into clean clothes. The dress I was wearing was soaked through with sweat and toxicity, and I felt that I could never wear it again. I ended up throwing it away, which immediately flooded me with relief.

When I woke up the next day, I could hear the hummingbirds zipping through the flowers, a sound I hadn't heard for years, even though they visited me often. As I went out back to stare at the garden, the woman who owned the house brought me a doll. It looked just like a doll I had when I was a child, one I had lost that was my favorite. As the woman handed her to me, she said, "Now you keep her, and don't lose her again." At that moment, I knew I had to fight to find my way back to myself, and that my life was a co-creation between my physical vessel here on earth and my connection to the Divine, which not everyone is always able to hear. Unintentionally, that began my sobriety journey in 2016.

It's a strange road to navigate when you want connection and people to tell you you're not alone. I understand that I'm not alone. I know I've been surrounded by beings my whole life. But there is a desire for real connection—to have relationships with people who get you, understand you, and don't discard you. People who love you when you're suddenly not perfect. I have yet to have much of that experience of unconditional love with humans, although I did with my grandmother Theresa (my mom's mom) and Frank. For that, I am grateful, because I know that it is possible and will happen again. I am also eternally humbled for having this divine connection to the sounds, voices, and energies with the holy of the holies, because even though I have fought it, intentionally forgotten, or resisted, it's kept me alive this entire time. Finally, I want to live for the first time in my life.

conclusion

A final thought on traversing the physical as a liminal
spirit in a human vessel . . .

IT'S IMPORTANT TO REMEMBER THAT WHILE you cannot change the past, you can redirect the future. Notice that I said "redirect" and not "control." There is a call and response to life that requires us to dance with it. Sometimes circumstances will take the lead, and you have to follow. This is not me telling you to give up, especially in the face of cruelty. What I am trying to tell you is that sometimes circumstances will be beyond your means to change.

Then there will be other times when you will be guided, or even pushed, to create the next steps without instruction—no support, no cheerleading, no reference point to look to for assurance. It will sometimes feel unfair to be told to change the world but not be told how. Without direct guidance or even the most basic encouragement, there will be days when the only clear examples of what to do next will be how *not* to do it. You may feel despair, or even resignation. There will be days when you will feel downright helpless and so dark in your spirit that leaving this earthly plane seems like the only solution. I can only say that those moments are natural but do pass. Sometimes it takes a few hours or days, and sometimes it can even take months on end. While it seems impossible to see the end of those periods while you're in them, fortunately, they do eventually pass.

And as you venture forth, my best wishes accompany you as you discover your path as a liminal being. Unlike those handed a predetermined route to success or a designated place in the tapestry of existence, you have a unique journey of freedom and exploration. Though this autonomy might sometimes induce fear, a sense of isolation, or the absence of support, I want you to know that I, and others who share your transformative journey, perceive your presence. We yearn for your well-being and embrace you with kindness as you navigate the complexities of this world. Despite the fear it might bring, please recognize that kindred souls and I see and support you.

Your story is yours to write, bearing the legacy of your lineage and diverse incarnations of your spirit. Let it be known that you possess the ability to forge your narrative, distinct from the norm, and you hold within you the remarkable privilege of preserving the stories of your lineage and the diverse manifestations of your soul. I urge you to tap into the energies of those before you and weave their aspirations into your tapestry of existence. In doing so, you'll find channels to express both their deepest yearnings and your highest self's vision.

As you continue, remember that you are not alone in your journey. Others like you stand in solidarity, weaving their threads into the grand design of existence. Embrace the camaraderie this brings. It is your story to tell and an ode to the evolution of spirit and the legacy of your lineage. May your journey be revitalizing, revolutionary, and replenishing, and may your heart find solace in the beauty of your unique narrative, so you may thrive as you celebrate all and who you are with the world around you.

recommended reading

The following books have helped me immensely on my journey back to myself, and continue to inspire my waking daily existence.

Belonging: Remembering Ourselves Home by Toko-pa Turner

Women Who Run with the Wolves: Myths and Stories of the Wild Woman Archetype by Clarissa Pinkola Estés

The Power of Vulnerability by Brené Brown

The Four Agreements: A Practical Guide to Personal Freedom by Don Miguel Ruiz

The Artist's Way by Julia Cameron

The 50th Law by 50 Cent and Robert Greene

The Laws of Spirit: A Tale of Transformation by Dan Millman

acknowledgments

I would like to acknowledge both my elevated and unwell ancestors. I would like to thank them for guiding me through these invisible spaces and places whether I've known them in the physical or not. I would like to acknowledge Adriana Stimola and Kate Zimmermann for believing in me and this work. I would like to acknowledge all of the growing pains throughout all the many lifetimes I've lived in this one vessel, for bribing me to keep going even when I didn't want to. I would like to acknowledge all of my benefic and malefic teachers, as you are one and the same. And finally but certainly not least I would like to thank the collective spirit of humanity and those beings of the liminal for transcending and traversing forever inspiring that new realities are always possible.

about the author

MARCELLA KROLL is a true multihyphenate. She is a multiracial, autistic artist, intuitive, spiritual teacher, and author with a thriving career in tarot readings and guidance since 2009. For fourteen years, she exclusively taught Tarot for Teens at the Los Angeles Public Library. Renowned for her mystical and ethereal artwork exhibited nationwide, Marcella blends tarot, astrology, and divination tools in her intuitive consultations. Her tarot decks are celebrated for their unique symbolism and stunning artwork. Her teachings focus on self-care, self-discovery, and intuition for personal transformation, and she offers courses and workshops on spirituality, magic, and personal growth. As the podcast host of *Saved by the Spell*, she delves into various topics and conducts expert interviews. Her artwork appears in the Rhode Island School of Design Museum's permanent collection and notable works like *Priestess* and Taschen's *Tarot* in the Library of Esoterica series. Marcella's contributions inspire spiritual connections and personal growth in today's ever-evolving world.